W9-BCL-178

DISCARDED
JENKS LRC
GORDON COLLEGE

THE GREEN FUSE

THE GREEN FUSE

An Ecological Odyssey

JOHN HARTE

Illustrations by Len Kamp

UNIVERSITY OF CALIFORNIA PRESS
Berkeley / Los Angeles / London

JENKS L.R.C.
GORDON COLLEGE
255 GRAPEVINE RD.
WENHAM, MA 01984-1895

QH
541.145
.H36
1993

The publisher gratefully acknowledges permission to use "The force that through the green fuse drives the flower," from Dylan Thomas, *Poems of Dylan Thomas,* copyright 1939 by New Directions Publishing Company. Reprinted by permission of New Directions.

University of California Press
Berkeley and Los Angeles, California

University of California Press
London, England

Copyright © 1993 by The Regents of the University of California

Library of Congress Cataloging-in-Publication Data
Harte, John, 1939–
The green fuse: an ecological odyssey / John Harte.
p. cm.
Includes bibliographical references and index.
ISBN 0–520–08207–9 (alk. paper)
1. Ecology. I. Title.
QH541.145.H36 1993 92–43115
574.5—dc20 CIP

Printed in the United States of America

1 2 3 4 5 6 7 8 9

The paper used in this publication meets the minimum requirements of American National Standard for Information Sciences—Permanence of Paper for Printed Library Materials, ANSI Z39.48–1984 ♾

For Julia, in her green age

The force that through the green fuse drives the flower
Drives my green age; that blasts the roots of trees
Is my destroyer.
And I am dumb to tell the crooked rose
My youth is bent by the same wintry fever.

The force that drives the water through the rocks
Drives my red blood; that dries the mouthing streams
Turns mine to wax.
And I am dumb to mouth unto my veins
How at the mountain spring the same mouth sucks.

The hand that whirls the water in the pool
Stirs the quicksand; that ropes the blowing wind
Hauls my shroud sail.
And I am dumb to tell the hanging man
How of my clay is made the hangman's lime.

The lips of time leech to the fountain head;
Love drips and gathers, but the fallen blood
Shall calm her sores.
And I am dumb to tell a weather's wind
How time has ticked a heaven round the stars.

And I am dumb to tell the lover's tomb
How at my sheet goes the same crooked worm.

—Dylan Thomas

Contents

ACKNOWLEDGMENTS

I thank Ian Baldwin, Paul Ehrlich, Gary Entsminger, Hilary Goldstine, Alexis Harte, Ken Harte, Ann Kinzig, Elizabeth Knoll, Mimi Sheiner, Jim Williams, and an anonymous reviewer for their critical reading of early versions of the manuscript. Because this book builds on the tremendous advances of recent decades in environmental science, I am indebted to my professional colleagues, who are too numerous to name, for the wealth of knowledge they have unearthed. Working with my graduate students from the Energy and Resources Group at the University of California, Berkeley, over the past eighteen years has also been an invaluable part of my education, and so I owe special thanks to Charles Blanchard, Asa Bradman, Brian Feifarek, Peter Gleick, Andrew Gunther, Erika Hoffman, Deborah Jensen, Kersten Johnson, Laura King, Ann Kinzig, Jim Kirchner, Daniel Lashof, Sharad Lele, Neo Martinez, Philippe Martin, Harvey Michaels, Dick Schneider, Becky Shaw, Karin Shen, Christine Shirley, Kathy Tonnessen, Margaret Torn, Matthew Turner, and Jim Williams. Financial support from the Pew Charitable Trusts greatly expedited the completion of this book, as did the superb copyediting by Sheila Berg and the overall management of production by the University of California Press. Elizabeth Knoll of that Press has once again provided me with invaluable encouragement and with advice that has greatly improved the book. Len Kamp deserves special thanks for turning my mediocre photos into evocative drawings. Stimulating collaborations over the past twenty-five years with Robert Socolow have left an indelible mark on this book, especially chapter 2. To Susan Lohr and all the others who make the Rocky Mountain Biological Laboratory such a splendid and inspiring place to do research and write, I am deeply grateful. In most of the field adventures described here, Mary Ellen Harte has been traipsing by my side or swimming ahead; during the writing, she has followed behind with red pencil and occasionally shovel. I owe to her more than words can express.

Prologue

The word "fuse" has many meanings, and all are appropriate here. One such meaning is a safety device that pops when the circuits are overloaded, a weak link in a system that serves as an early warning signal. Often the image of a caged canary in a mine is invoked to illustrate such a warning system. When the canary fainted from gas fumes, the miners knew it was time to flee the mine to avoid the same fate. In the context of planetary abuse, however, the canary image is inadequate. Humanity has no place to run. It is not our prerogative to flee but, rather, our duty to fix—to unplug the source of the overload and rethink the way the whole system is operating. A variety of circuit-overload fuses are described here, some prosaically underfoot and others in exotic places.

In another sense, fuses are slow-burning devices used to ignite explosions. Inadvertently, we are lighting such fuses around the planet. Some are green and literally burning, like the forests of the tropics. Others, like the pollution of our skies and waters, are tantamount to a lit fuse, because the consequences they will unleash will dramatically overshadow in both tempo and magnitude the triggering events—consequences such as an explosive deterioration in the quality of life for our grandchildren.

Finally, "to fuse" means to combine, unite, join. The oneness or unity of nature has been a theme of poets and philosophers for millennia. The unity of the laws of nature has been a theme of science since Galileo. Physicists have demonstrated that the laws of motion hold true on spaceships and distant stars as well as in earth's laboratories. Biologists have taught us that the same DNA-encoded information-processing system is used by the genes of bacteria, worms, roses, ravens, and human beings.

Is there such unity among the diverse places and processes that comprise our global ecosystem? In the conventional view of life on earth, biologically rich and special places like the Amazon Basin, the Everglades, and the Great Barrier Reef are like animals in a zoo—each in its cage to be watched and enjoyed as we stroll past. An understanding of the *intra*dependencies, the linkages within any of those ecosystems, can be gleaned from books, nature documentaries on film, and firsthand observation. But the *inter*dependencies, the linkages among such distant places and their relation to our everyday lives, are more difficult to observe. Thus, the conventional caged-animal view prevails.

The unity that emerges from the findings of ecology and other earth sciences today is a profound one, and it has shattered this conventional view of isolated ecosystems. It also teaches us that we are not casual zoo visitors, strolling by the splendid vistas, but rather that our lives and well-being are mutually dependent on—fused with—those of the bacteria in the soil, the shrubs in a remote tropical forest, the salamanders crawling on muddy pond bottoms.

Touch one strand, and the whole web shivers. The pages that follow offer a glimpse of the pervasiveness, the economic importance, and the lovely magic of this global fusion.

1

A Walk up Hidden Creek

The salmon carcasses carpeting both banks of Hidden Creek had been deftly decerebrated, and only careful footwork prevented us from stepping on them. Feeling like disrespectful witnesses to some foreign rite, we worked our way slowly upstream along the left bank to a gravel-bottomed headwater pond, darkened amid a thick grove of poplar trees. Here, in the red and sputtering pond water, was a frenzied mass of live salmon, while around the shore there sprawled yet more fish with gaping hollow brain cavities. The hideous litter of a mad surgeon? Certainly a fast-moving one, for the appearance of a few of the bodies suggested a recent death, probably within minutes of our trespass, and yet no killer was in sight. Most, though, had met their strange fate long enough ago for cloaks of maggots to have adorned their corpses.

The freshly killed ones especially piqued our interest, because we suspected that lurking nearby—probably just out of sight in the tall grass right above us—was *Ursus arctos*, commonly called the grizzly bear. It was late summer in southwestern Alaska, when the bears are on a prehibernation binge to store up winter fat. Glia cells, which constitute most of an animal's brain except for the "wires," are particularly rich in fat and thus offer a fine food source. Fortunately for the bears, fishing at this time of year is as easy as slurping honey from a bucket; with each paw swipe through the salmon-filled water, a bear can invariably snatch a ten-pounder.

The thought that a grizzly would find our skulls little more of a barrier to the delicacy within than that of a salmon was hard to suppress. But since the bears were eating only the salmon brains and leaving most of the flesh to rot, we were reassured that food was abundant for them. Fear of us, perhaps, but not hunger might precipitate an attack. So we walked up along Hidden Creek ringing our bear bells and chanting "Hey bear! Hey bear!" now and then to signal our presence and avoid surprising one.

Earlier that day, downstream in Brooks Lake, we had seen some small salmon, "fingerlings," and now we were seeing these swirling masses of large salmon but none of an in-between size. It was as though we had encountered a village in which there lived only small children and dying old folks. Why?

The reason is simple. The fertilized eggs of the salmon produce hatchlings that grow for two or three years in Brooks Lake. At that time, still quite small, the surviving fingerlings swim out to sea. Three or four years later and ten pounds heavier, the oceanic survivors, several thousand mature sockeye salmon, return to Brooks Lake to spawn. From Bristol Bay, they swim up the Naknek River to Naknek Lake and into the Brooks River, where they must leap a five-foot falls before arriving at Brooks Lake. Once in Brooks Lake, they select Hidden Creek or one of the four others like it that flow there from forest or tundra. Each fish is instinctively drawn by chemical cues to the very creek where it had earlier hatched from an egg laid and fertilized by a pair of spawning salmon. Like their parents six years before, each returning salmon is at the end of its life. The waters were red that day at Hidden Creek, not with blood but with the crimson shades of dying salmon. With their innards rotting, their jaws grown bony and protuberant, and their nerves and hormones united for the final purpose of procreation, the weary salmon probably did not see the morrow dawn.

Our trip to Hidden Creek was more prosaic than the salmon's. Unable to navigate chemically or leap waterfalls, we came in by floatplane to Naknek Lake and then followed a Katmai National Park maintenance road along the Brooks River to Brooks Lake. From there, we canoed across Brooks Lake to the mouth of Hidden Creek. A salmon-fattened bald eagle chick screamed for its dinner from a nest high in a dead tree at the mouth of the creek. At the sandy shoreline, where the

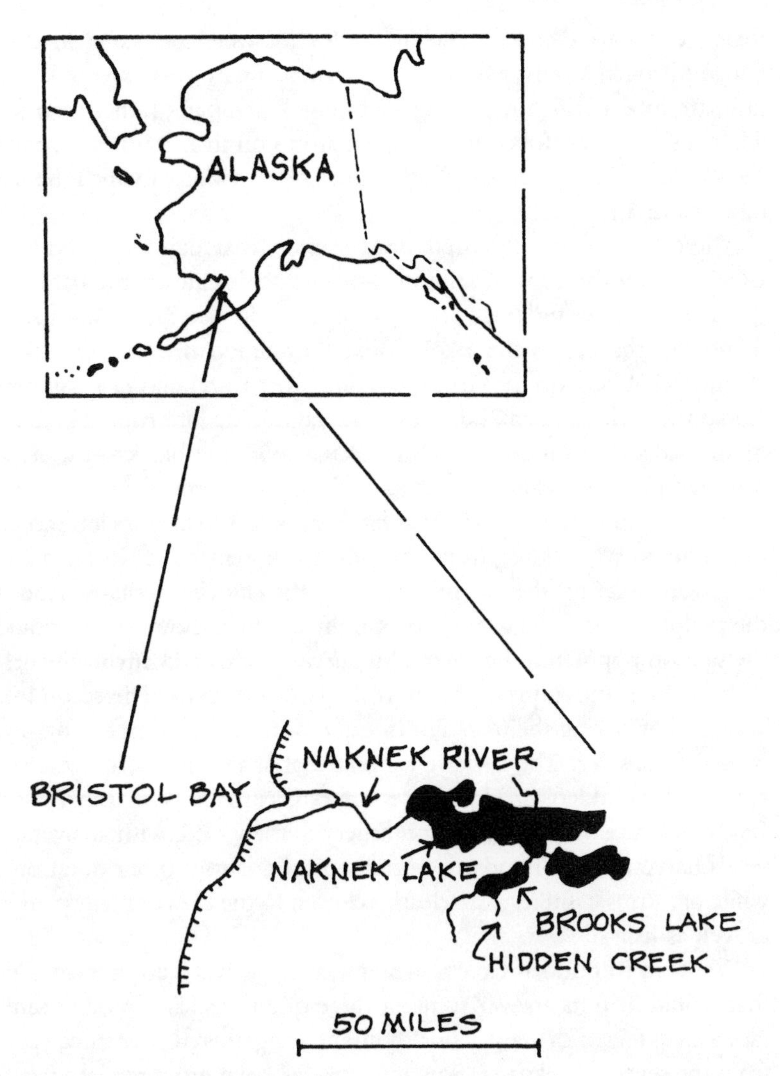

creek turns and slices sideways behind a sandbar of its own making, the fiery waters flashed. Here, we first saw the reddened salmon in large masses as they writhed upstream, intent only on reaching a gravel bed in the headwater pond where they would release sperm or eggs from their deformed and dying bodies. That darkened glade, where the salmon's journey begins and ends, intimates sanctity and the gift of life in all its profusion and wildness.

The eye-catching salmon corpses were nose-catching as well, and our purpose that day had to do with certain molecules of which they, and their stench, were made. The molecules we were interested in contained nitrogen atoms. Niggling over atomic innards may seem like the ultimate in scientific nit-picking—looking at the parts rather than the whole fish—but by following nitrogen atoms on their journey through the Alaskan waters, we may glimpse the larger system, of which the salmon is but a part.[1]

There were many hundred dead salmon that day along Hidden Creek. Could the tons of salmon chowder oozing down the banks of the little meandering creek and flowing into the lake be of any harm, or use, to the life in the lake? Could the salmon rot alter the lake's chemistry? Where do the chemicals come from to rebuild new salmon? Could the cycle of life and death for the salmon be interrupted because of an inadequate supply of life's molecular building blocks—the same way that farmers' fields can become infertile over time as nutrients are used up? Although Brooks Lake is far from industrialized society, could the pollutants generated from afar affect this remote environment in some way, altering the air, the water, or the climate, perhaps? And if the pollutants do have some sort of influence here, how robust would the salmon population be? Would it survive a changed environment?

In science, most questions are really two questions. The second is, why are you asking the first? For our questions, the accompanying one is easy to answer. The sockeye salmon that spawn in the network of creeks, like Hidden Creek, whose waters eventually flow into Bristol Bay, constitute the largest salmon fishery in the world, with an average year's harvest worth hundreds of millions of dollars. So our questions, while of intrinsic interest, are clearly relevant to the lives of many people as well as fish.

We went to Hidden Creek, in summer 1984, to take water samples that would help us answer some of these questions. These water samples were a few of the nearly one thousand we gathered over three years from the several creeks that flow into Brooks Lake, from the lake itself, from the Brooks and Naknek rivers, and from rain- and snowstorms that might be bringing pollution in from afar. In the technical jargon of ecologists, we were gathering data to determine the "nitrogen budget" for Brooks Lake. Like an accountant keeping track of where the money comes and goes in a company's budget, we wanted to know how the nitrogen comes into and goes out of an Alaskan lake; like the

1. I have unabashedly borrowed the image of an "atom's journey" from Aldo Leopold's *A Sand County Almanac* (Oxford: Oxford University Press, 1941).

company owners, we wanted the information to learn more about the overall health of the enterprise. Andrew Gunther, then my graduate student in the Energy and Resources Group at the University of California, Berkeley, designed and conducted the three-year research effort for his doctoral dissertation.

To sharpen the questions and to understand the way we went about trying to answer them, we must take a short detour to learn about the ingredients of life. Within a lake or forest or, indeed, any ecosystem, there are accumulations of wealth. In much the same way that the wealth of talent, traditions, and resources in a community or nation provides an indication of how it will cope with stresses and how long it can endure in its present form, so, too, does ecological wealth provide a measure of natural robustness.

Ecological wealth takes many forms. There is, for instance, genetic wealth, characterized by a wide variety of species and, within a species, by a wide variety of individual genetic strains. Genetic wealth is of value to a species because it increases the likelihood that at least some of its members will survive hard times.

Consider, for example, climate stress. Evidence exists that the world is warming, and our current understanding of how climate works suggests that this trend will continue for another century. This change in the global climate is likely to be particularly severe in Alaska and elsewhere in the high latitudes. If the gene pool of the salmon that spawn at Hidden Creek contains only genes that enable the fish to cope with the present climate, then the Hidden Creek salmon population probably could not survive a dramatic change in climate. And if enough populations do not survive, then the species could even become extinct. With greater genetic diversity, the odds increase that at least some of the salmon will have the right genes to enable them to survive the changing climatic conditions and be the parents of a future population.

Genetic wealth is also of direct material value to human society. From the existing variety of wild species and the variety of genetic types within a species, people have obtained lifesaving medicines and hardier seeds for agriculture. Thus, the genes of each wild species not only help that species to survive but are also part of the life-support system for other species, including our own.

Ecological wealth is also stored in certain key elements in waters, soils, and living tissue. Whereas genes provide the information—the blueprint—needed to construct the organism, these elements are the building blocks. The elements most abundant in living tissue are carbon, hydrogen, and oxygen. In the process of photosynthesis, green plants use the sun's energy to make energy-rich sugars from carbon dioxide and water. Carbon dioxide (a gas present in air and water) contains carbon and oxygen, while water is made of hydrogen and oxygen. By subsequently breaking down the photosynthesized sugars, plants derive the energy needed to grow. Animals obtain their energy from the plants on which they graze or, if they are carnivores, from other animals. Even for the carnivores, however, if you trace the diet back far enough, you generally find that all of the energy that animals derive from food ultimately comes from sunlight and plant photosynthesis.

Among the few exceptions are certain deep-sea ecosystems to which little sunlight penetrates. The role of green plants in these ecosystems is played by microorganisms that derive their energy by breaking down energy-rich chemicals emerging from volcanic fissures in the seabed. But while there are exceptions to the general rule that sunlight is the source of energy that powers life, there is no exception to a finding of physics that dictates how energy is used within ecosystems. This finding, the second law of thermodynamics, tells us that energy, unlike material, cannot be completely recycled. Thus, there can be no ecosystem, anywhere, in which meat eaters just eat each other, simply recycling the energy. Such a "perpetual motion ecosystem" would not need the sun or some other external energy source to power it; its existence would contradict this fundamental and time-tested law of physics.

Carbon, hydrogen, and oxygen are not the only essential building blocks of life, however, for no living thing can be constructed of sugar alone. Even the chlorophyll molecule, the green plant's machinery that allows it to tap sunlight and make sugar, cannot be made simply of sugars; it must contain nitrogen and trace amounts of certain metals. Other important pieces of life, such as the ATP molecule (which permits plants and animals to make effective use of energy), must contain the element phosphorus. Both nitrogen and phosphorus are necessary to make genes. And sulfur is necessary to provide rigidity to proteins; without that element in our bodies, our flesh would hang on our bones like a jellyfish on a coat hanger.

Elements like nitrogen, phosphorus, and sulfur are called nutrients. An animal obtains nutrients, such as nitrogen, prepackaged in the organic molecules of its food. These organic molecules are generally fairly complex structures, sometimes containing tens or hundreds of atoms, mostly carbon and hydrogen but also various nutrients. In contrast, plants obtain their nutrients from inorganic substances. Inorganic molecules are generally simpler than organic ones and do not contain both carbon and hydrogen. For instance, the nitrogen taken up by a stalk of grass is most likely to be either some form of ammonia (a simple molecule composed of three hydrogen atoms and one nitrogen atom) or nitrate (composed of three oxygen atoms and one nitrogen atom).

The major source of nitrogen for plants is the decay of dead plants and animals that occurs when bacteria and fungi digest the corpses. In the process of decay, complex organic forms of nitrogen, such as proteins, are broken down into simpler inorganic types that serve as fertilizers for plants. And so we speak of a "nitrogen cycle," to express the fact that in an ecosystem, nitrogen is converted from an inorganic chemical nutrient to organic form (such as living plant tissue) and thence, on the death of the organism, back to an inorganic form, which is taken up by plants again.

The cycle is not a perfect one, however, for there are places along the cycle where nitrogen may exit or enter it. Consider, for example, a forest on the slope of a hill. Rainfall will dissolve some of the nitrogen from the soil and wash it downhill, perhaps into a lake. If either forest or lake is viewed in isolation, its nitrogen cycle would not be viewed as closed: the forest suffers a net loss of nitrogen, while the lake receives a subsidy of nitrogen from the forest. Even the two systems lumped together and viewed as one may gain or lose. For example, a flock of geese may arrive at the lake, defecate, and thereby augment its supply of nitrogen. The birds might have obtained this nitrogen from some place far away where they had their last meal (and where there will then result a net loss of nitrogen).

If soil or water lacks adequate nutrients, plant growth will be stunted. In lakes and in seas, the most productive photosynthesizers are the one-celled organisms called phytoplankton. If they do not grow, then neither can the very tiny animals, called zooplankton, that graze on the phytoplankton. And without the zooplankton, there would be no small shrimp and other fingernail-sized forms of animal life, the food of the young salmon. Thus, in a few years, there would be no returning adult salmon to spawn; the salmon population would soon die out. And so would, ultimately, the bears. Moreover, the gigantic commercial salmon fishing industry would collapse. In short, a vital food chain would topple at its base because of lack of nutrients.

If an ecosystem contains only small quantities of nitrogen but has abundant amounts of all the other nutrients necessary for plant growth, then it is called nitrogen limited. Add nitrogen, and you will stimulate growth. By essentially doing just that—adding nitrogen to jars of Brooks Lake water and measuring the increase in phytoplankton growth—Charles Goldman, a lake ecologist at the University of California, Davis, discovered in the 1950s that the lake was, in fact, nitrogen limited.

Stunted plants on nitrogen-poor soil or in a nitrogen-limited lake are like starving beggars just outside the locked gates to a mansion. For surrounding all life on earth is a pool of nitrogen that is huge beyond all needs. This is the nitrogen gas in the atmosphere, a pool that is several hundred thousand times larger than the entire amount of nitrogen in all of the planet's living vegetation—certainly plenty for all. But in a plight similar to that of the beggars, most plants lack the key to unlock this treasure. The nitrogen in the atmosphere is not bound to hydrogen or oxygen and therefore cannot be used by the majority of plants. The exception is a group of plants, called legumes, that host a special group of microorganisms that are capable of turning the atmospheric nitrogen into fertilizer nitrogen in a process called nitrogen fixation. Peas, soybeans, and alfalfa are common domesticated legumes. They play a very important role in agriculture because they reduce the need to throw expensive fertilizers on the soil. Other nitrogen-fixing organisms exist, such as some types of blue-green algae, which need no host plant. Nitrogen-fixing algae sometimes team up with fungus to form nitrogen-fixing lichens. Occurring in a dazzling array of colors and forms, lichens are truly unusual forms of life, for they are species composed of other species.[2] They are often able to survive harsher environments than other organisms because the algal and fungal constituents provide complementary benefits (photosynthesis and possibly nitrogen fixation by the algae, extraction of phosphorus and other nutrients from dead plant matter by the fungus).

Nature has also provided a symmetrically reverse process called denitrification. Like nitrogen fixation, this, too, is carried out by microorganisms. These denitrifying bacteria transform nitrogen that is in the form of a nutrient in soil or water into nitrogen gases that go into the atmosphere. One of the gaseous products of denitrification is molecular

2. Beatrix Potter, the writer and original illustrator of the Peter Rabbit books, was the first person to unravel the mystery of the lichens. Scientists at the time did not take seriously her idea that lichens were an association of two types of well-known organisms, and even her meticulous drawings based on microscope studies failed to convince the male-chauvinistic scientific profession of nineteenth-century England. Discouraged from a career in botany, she turned to writing childrens' stories.

nitrogen gas—the same stuff that occupies about four-fifths of the atmosphere. Another is called nitrous oxide or, in common parlance, laughing gas. This gas is no laughing matter, however, for it affects how much cancer-causing ultraviolet radiation from the sun reaches the surface of the earth (see chap. 5) and also influences our climate (see chap. 2).

The more one looks at the many roles nitrogen plays in nature, the more interesting this common, light element seems. Indeed, nitrogen is the Jekyll and Hyde of chemicals:

- As a plant fertilizer, under conditions where nitrogen is naturally scarce in soil, it is Dr. Jekyll. But where drinking water contains too much nitrogen from fertilizer-laden farm runoff, causing a blood disease called methemoglobinemia that can be fatal in infants, it is Mr. Hyde.
- As a food preservative in the form of nitrates and nitrites, it prevents botulism. But when those same preservatives in our foods form nitrosamines, which are powerful cancer-causing substances, it is a hazard.
- As a scavenger of chlorine, nitrogen partially protects the stratospheric ozone shield from the devastating effects of chlorofluorocarbons and thereby protects us from ultraviolet radiation. But as ozone-destroying nitric oxide in the stratosphere, it has the opposite effect.
- As a crucial ingredient of proteins, it is essential to life. But as a key constituent of the nitric acid in acid rain, and as a crucial chemical agent in the formation of urban smog, it is a hazard to life.
- As an ingredient in the manufacture of glass, it brings us many benefits. But it is also a necessary ingredient of gunpowder.

Returning to Alaska, what are the sources of nitrogen to Brooks Lake? The salmon returning from the sea to spawn and die bring nitrogen to the lake—the nitrogen in their bodies, which came from the marine life on which they fattened at sea. Some of this nitrogen would enter the lake via its tributaries, like Hidden Creek, where the salmon die in great numbers. Nitrogen fixation by algae in the lake could also be a source, as could nitrogen fixation by organisms growing on the hillsides above the lake as some of that fixed nitrogen might wash into the lake. Nitrogen dissolved in rain- and snowfall is another. This is not so farfetched, at least in places where acid rain occurs, because nitric acid, an important constituent of acid rain, contains nitrogen. Thus, atmospheric pollution from automobiles in faraway cities could be a source of new, fertilizing nitrogen in Brooks Lake. The decay of dead plants and animals that grew in the lake is also a source of nitrogen for aquatic plant growth, but it adds no *new* nitrogen because the fertilizing nitrogen is simply recycled during this process.

What about the losses? First, nitrogen can exit, dissolved or suspended, in the Brooks River water that flows out of Brooks Lake and ultimately to sea. Second, the two- to three-year-old salmon heading out to sea each year take their corpuscular nitrogen with them. Although they are much smaller than the returning adults, the fingerlings are far more numerous, so this loss of nitrogen has to be considered in the budget. Finally, denitrification leaks nitrogen into the atmosphere, resulting in a loss from the lake and the surrounding soils.

For the nitrogen to be in balance, the sources must equal the sinks, not necessarily day by day but at least over periods of many years. If all the sinks and sources could be plugged, we would have what ecologists call a closed cycle. Like a bank account that remains unchanged because there are no deposits and withdrawals, the amounts of chemicals in the water would never change. But, in fact, there is nitrogen fixation going on rather actively in this watershed: fish do come and go, rain and snow do deposit some nitrogen, and Brooks River does drain a considerable amount of nitrogen out of the watershed. So how does the system remain in balance year after year, or does it? And what role do the salmon play? We are back to our old questions, but they are now sharpened to the point where we can go about answering them.

Let us start with the salmon. Do the fingerlings heading out to sea remove from the watershed more or less nitrogen than is added to the watershed by the smaller number of larger returning salmon each year? Consider the salmon's life cycle. Although each adult female that successfully spawns will lay about a thousand eggs, most eggs are defective or get eaten by trout, predatory insects, and other scavenging animals that can slurp them up off the gravelly spawning beds. Only about one hundred of the thousand eggs are likely to hatch and produce healthy salmon fry. During the first two to three years of a hatchling's life, there is a premium on growing fast because the littlest fry make the easiest prey for the large rainbow trout that cruise Brooks Lake, pruning the salmon population mercilessly.

If we follow a typical group of the hundred sockeye salmon hatchlings from an individual female's clutch of eggs, we would find that only about ten of the hundred will survive the rigors of freshwater life. At the end of two or three years, however, these ten surviving fingerlings will head out to sea. They are what the commercial fish harvesters call out-migrants. Thus, from the thousand eggs laid by one adult female salmon, roughly ten three-ounce salmon will out-migrate. Several years and ten pounds later, the urge to spawn triggers a journey back upstream to the site where they were born. However, of the ten brothers and sisters, only about half will survive at sea; the other half succumb to a combination of commercial fishers and natural predators.

For these remaining five salmon from the original batch of one female's eggs, the return to their spawning grounds poses further hazards. Of the five, roughly three are unable to flip up over the waterfalls that they encounter on the way to the spawning grounds, and they simply die of old age, deprived of their one chance to reproduce. Only about one in twenty salmon are pawed up out of the water by a hungry grizzly, and so the chances of one of our five becoming bear meat are small. With even lower odds, some salmon will fail to escape the clutches of eager sportfishermen, who have traveled a thousand miles or more to match wits with the doomed fish. Thus, on the average, about two salmon will return to spawn from a batch of one thousand eggs laid by an individual female sockeye. Of those two survivors, on average one is female, and she will lay on average another thousand eggs. And so the cycle of the salmon continues.

Now we can figure out whether there is a net import or export of salmon flesh to Brooks Lake. Each year about twenty thousand three-ounce salmon out-migrate from Brooks Lake. That means roughly two tons of fish exit the lake. But also each year, about four thousand adult salmon arrive at the lake to spawn and die. They each weigh about ten pounds, so that works out to about twenty tons of fish entering the lake from the sea. Thus, working out the fish budget, we see that each year there is a net gain to Brooks Lake of nearly twenty tons of fish flesh, which, it turns out, contain about a quarter of a ton of nitrogen.

Could any other animals either import or export comparable amounts of nitrogen? No large flocks of geese, ducks, or other wetland birds were in evidence, so bird droppings probably do not play a significant role in the nitrogen cycle. But a glance at a cruising hawk owl swooping low over the tundra to snatch a red vole recalled an observation made earlier in the day. Along one shoreline of Brooks Lake, be-

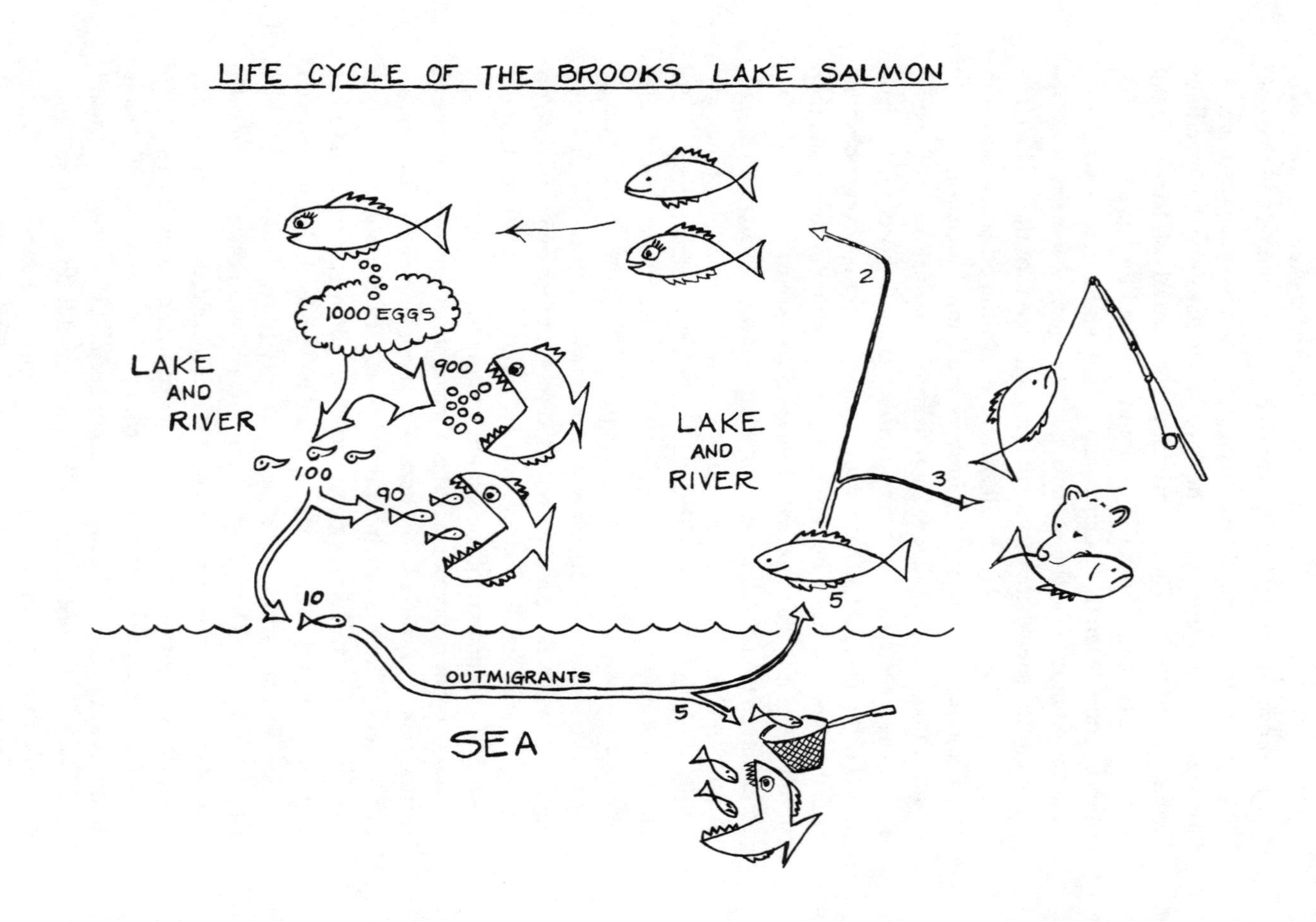
LIFE CYCLE OF THE BROOKS LAKE SALMON
1000 EGGS
LAKE AND RIVER
900
100
90
10
LAKE AND RIVER
2
3
5
OUTMIGRANTS
5
SEA

low an embankment, we saw what we estimated to be thousands of these tiny rodents, dead. The red vole is a close relative of the lemmings of the Scandinavian arctic that are notorious for their putative suicidal plunges off cliffs. Could the voles we saw have committed suicide by jumping off the enbankment? And could their corpses significantly augment the lake's nitrogen supply? To the first question, the answer is, hardly, for the bank was only three feet high. The voles had surely drowned in the lake, probably because population pressure had compelled those without breeding territory to seek new frontiers across the lake. Their corpses were then washed up on the shoreline. Thinking about the numbers of dead voles on the shoreline, the amount of time a corpse remains there, and the amount of nitrogen in each one convinced us that the voles contribute to the lake's nitrogen supply only a small fraction of what the returning salmon do.

Does this mean that Brooks Lake is being steadily enriched with nitrogen? Or does nitrogen leak out of the lake at the same rate it comes in via dying salmon? An obvious first place to look for such a "leakage" is the Brooks River—the stream that drains Brooks Lake's waters into Naknek Lake. The amount of nitrogen exported via Brooks River each year can be estimated by measuring the concentration of nitrogen in Brooks River. For example, if the river water contained on average one pound of nitrogen per million gallons, and the flow rate of the river was one thousand million gallons per year, then the export rate would be one thousand pounds of nitrogen per year. In this way, we determined that nitrogen is exported from Brooks Lake via the river at a rate of about ten tons per year. This far exceeds the net gain of a quarter of a ton of nitrogen from returning fish and tips the scales the opposite way: now the lake appears to be losing nitrogen each year.

So if the budget is to balance, there must be a compensating inflow. Is it possible that Hidden Creek and the five other streams that flow into Brooks Lake contain significantly more nitrogen than the several hundred pounds per year contributed by rotting salmon? The dense mass of dying salmon in the creek makes such a possibility hard to believe, but the only way to find out for sure is to measure the concentrations in these six streams. We did just that and found that impressions can, indeed, be deceiving. All the inflow streams, together, it turns out, contribute to Brooks Lake about ten tons of nitrogen per year, far more than the amount supplied by the salmon chowder. Considering the measurement errors that are inevitable in measuring the nitrogen contents and the water flow rates of these stream waters, the budget can be said to balance "within experimental error."

Now we have balanced the books on nitrogen and learned two things: the salmon are not important to the nitrogen budget, and the future supply of nitrogen for the growing salmon fry seems assured. Our job is done.

Or is it? Where does all the nitrogen that spills into Brooks Lake from the creeks come from? If the upland soils are being eroded or leached of their nitrogen, then this import to the lake may not last very long, and eventually, when it is exhausted, the lake's nitrogen levels will plummet and so will the numbers of salmon. Is there some source of nitrogen we have ignored that is replenishing the soils above the lake?[3]

Of course, there is—and we have already referred to it in passing—nitrogen fixation. The lush beds of the lichen *Peltigera* in the low-lying spruce forest, the brittle mats of another lichen, *Stereocaulen,* on the higher tundra, and, most of all, the thick stands of nitrogen-fixing alder trees along the lakeshore and on the lower slopes of Dumpling and Kelez mountains all contribute mightily to the annual nitrogen budget of the entire watershed. Since nobody had determined the role of these nitrogen-fixing organisms in the nitrogen cycle of the watershed, we set out to do so. For the lichens, this first meant conducting rather tedious censuses of lichen distribution in representative patches scattered within all the diverse types of habitat in the 200-square-mile watershed.

On hands and knees, swatting mosquitoes all the while, we did just that. From these censuses, combined with LANDSAT color satellite photos of watershed habitats and measurements of how fast nitrogen can be fixed by lichens, we deduced that roughly twenty tons of nitrogen are fixed by lichens annually in the watershed.[4] Adding to this an

3. A simple "back-of-the-envelope" estimate suggests that there must be. The argument goes as follows. The total stock of readily erodable organic and inorganic nitrogen in the upland soils is a few thousand tons. If the soils are sending 10 tons of nitrogen each year to Brooks Lake, and the soil nitrogen is not replenished, then the stock could last no longer than a few hundred years. But the lake has nearly certainly been a productive salmon nursery for far longer, and, if anything, the stock of nitrogen in the soils has been increasing since the last ice age. There must be some external source of nitrogen that replenishes the upland soils.

4. We measured the area of ground covered by nitrogen-fixing lichens in 50 large and randomly chosen patches throughout the watershed, representing spruce forest, high tundra slopes, and 8 other distinct habitats comprising the entire watershed. From this, we could estimate how much of each habitat is covered by the different nitrogen-fixing lichens. Using satellite pictures of the region, in which the various habitats are distinguished by their colors on infrared-sensitive film, we were able to estimate the area of

estimate of the even larger, but less well measured, contribution of the alder trees in the watershed, we arrived at a grand total input of roughly two hundred tons of nitrogen fixed from the atmosphere each year. This input to the watershed is much larger than the Brooks Lake nitrogen inflow or outflow rate. An unknown fraction of the two hundred tons per year fixed by lichen and alder is denitrified back to the atmosphere by soil microorganisms, but, nevertheless, the nitrogen fixation rate is so large that there is little reason to worry about whether the input to the lake will deplete the upland soils. The abundant stock of nitrogen in the atmosphere is sustaining the nitrogen budget in our lake.

Although the rate of nitrogen fixation in the watershed is large enough to sustain the nitrogen influx to the lake, it is small compared to yet another flow of nitrogen—a cyclic flow that does not involve atmospheric nitrogen at all. Within the soil and within Brooks Lake, the nitrogen in dead plant and animal matter is recycled back to a form in which plants can use it as a nutrient. This recycling (or turnover, as ecologists call it) of nitrogen is carried out by a host of bacteria and fungi; it is aided by earthworms, beetles, and other animals that chew up the dead matter to make it more accessible to the bacteria and fungi who often inhabit the feces of these animals. In the soils of the watershed, nitrogen turnover averages about two thousand tons per year (compared to 200 tons per year of nitrogen input from the atmosphere), while in Brooks Lake, turnover averages one hundred tons per year (compared to about 10 tons per year input from the creeks). So we see that the Brooks Lake watershed does a good job recycling, requiring an annual input subsidy equal to only about one-tenth of its turnover. Imagine being able to meet 90 percent of your material needs by recycling and only purchasing 10 percent from stores.

There are some ecosystems in which nitrogen supply for plant growth is more dependent on external subsidies than at Brooks Lake. In the tundra soils above the banks of the Colville River in northern Alaska, nitrogen fixation is not only the dominant source of nitrogen to the river, but it contributes significantly to the nitrogen enrichment

---

each habitat. Knowing how much of each area was covered by lichens and the sizes of the areas, we were able to calculate the total area of each species of nitrogen-fixing lichen throughout the entire watershed. For each species, we then measured the rate of nitrogen fixation by tiny pieces of lichen of predetermined area. Multiplying the rate per fixed area by the total area of each species, we then knew the total amount of nitrogen fixed by lichens each year in the watershed.

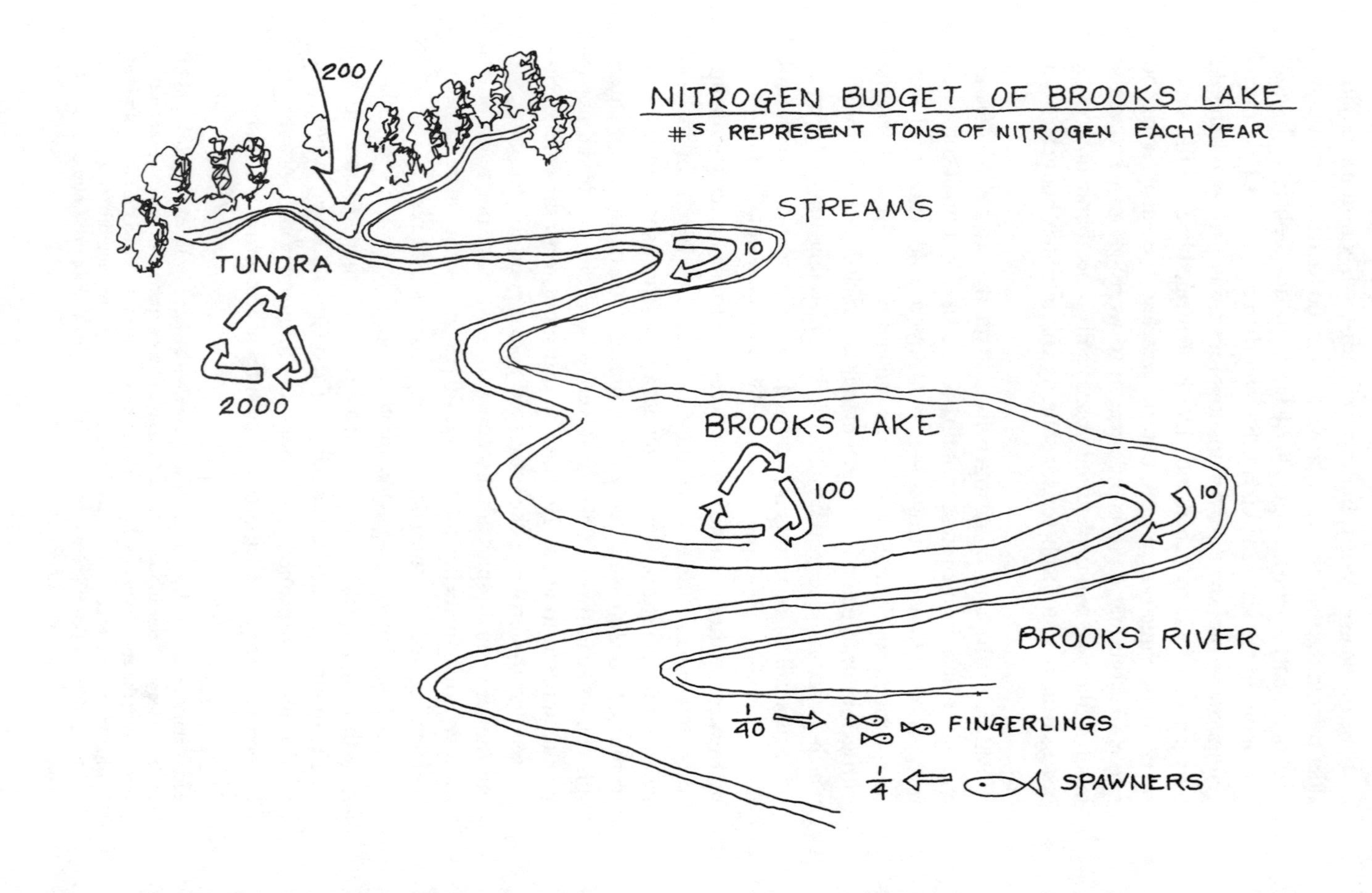
NITROGEN BUDGET OF BROOKS LAKE
#S REPRESENT TONS OF NITROGEN EACH YEAR
200
TUNDRA
2000
STREAMS
10
BROOKS LAKE
100
10
BROOKS RIVER
1/40
FINGERLINGS
1/4
SPAWNERS

of the coastal waters as well. Vera Alexander, an ecologist at the University of Alaska, has shown that lichens growing on the tundra at this site are a major source of nitrogen in the Beaufort Sea, into which the river drains.

In other places on earth where major rivers, such as the Amazon or the Mississippi, enter the sea, the amount of nitrogen entering marine waters vastly exceeds that in the arctic. Added up over all the rivers on earth, the global flow of nitrogen from land to sea currently totals roughly one hundred million tons a year. It is largely derived from eroded or leached soil lost irreversibly to the sea, and this flow rate has increased tenfold since prehistoric times because of erosion caused by human land mismanagement. A sizable portion of the "lost" nitrogen originated as chemical fertilizer on farmlands, and in principle, this can be replaced with additional fertilizer, although at considerable cost. But erosion also generally alters the fabric, or texture, of the soil left behind, and, as a result, the moisture-holding capability of the soil generally declines. Soil fabric is, in part, determined by the aged organic matter in the soil, and this cannot be replaced, at least on a time scale of a human lifetime, in any practical sense.

Is the eroded nitrogen influencing marine fertility in places other than the Beaufort Sea, where it is a purely natural phenomenon? A nitrogen budget of the oceans similar to that of Brooks Lake reveals that the input from all rivers is about the same as that from nitrogen fixation by marine organisms, but this amount is much less than that taken up each year by marine plants. Thus, on a global scale, the impact of the eroded nitrogen should be small. In some coastal waters, however, such as Chesapeake Bay and Everglades National Park, inputs of nitrogen from the land to the water are causing considerable ecological disruption.

Having gained confidence from our reconstruction of the Brooks Lake nitrogen budget that the sources of nitrogen to the soils of the watershed are adequate to explain the inflow of nitrogen to Brooks Lake—that the budget is not steadily going into a deficit—it looks this time like our job is really done. But, again, a nagging doubt remains. Could some environmental stress, such as pollution in the rain, damage the ability of the lichen and the alder to fix nitrogen and thus eventually throw the budget out of balance by reducing the input? Or might nitric acid, an ingredient of acid rain, increase the nitrogen inflow to the watershed? Nitric acid can be a menace in two different ways: the acid might directly poison life, or the nitrogen in nitric acid might overstimulate the growth of certain plants and thereby cause ecological changes.

It might seem unlikely that rain would be polluted here in remote Alaska. But, in fact, there is atmospheric pollution in the subarctic and arctic, right up to the North Pole in the Canadian and European arctic, as well as in northern Alaska. It is called arctic haze.

Since the mid-1970s, when its presence was first noted and publicized by Glenn Shaw of the University of Alaska, researchers from over a dozen nations have been mounting a major effort to understand its sources and its effects.[5] Much has now been learned about arctic haze from this effort. We know that the pollution consists of sulfuric acid, certain toxic metals such as lead, and carbon soot. The levels of atmospheric pollution begin to build up in the arctic air each autumn, reach a peak in late winter or early spring, and disappear by the middle of spring. At their peak, the pollutants are found at levels comparable to those occurring year-round in the air above moderately polluted cities such as Oakland, California. The soot in the springtime arctic air is enough to block out 5 to 10 percent of the arctic sunlight. All the industrialized nations of the Northern Hemisphere contribute to the pollution, and very little of it is actually generated within the arctic. In winter, the arctic air is, in effect, an atmospheric "dump" for these nations. Air pollutants tend to rain out over the ocean in winter, so the major atmospheric route by which the pollution reaches the arctic is over the Eurasian landmass.[6]

5. Airborne instruments that sample the atmospheric pollution have been flown by researchers halfway around the Pole, and numerous ground-based stations are gathering data on deposition of the pollution and on changes in atmospheric transparency. Up through 1991, nearly all the data on arctic haze has come from measurements by North American and Western European scientists in the western arctic. East-West collaboration to measure atmospheric pollution in the Siberian arctic (which comprises roughly half of all the world's arctic land and water) is likely to begin in the early 1990s, a scientific spinoff of glasnost and the events it unleashed.

6. While the United States produces about 30 percent of all the world's air pollution, it only contributes about 10 percent of the arctic haze. U.S. pollution tends to rain out over the United States itself or over the North Atlantic before reaching the arctic. Thus, the share of the arctic pollution that the United States contributes is less than might be expected, based on its total industrial activity. Pollution from the former Soviet Union and parts of Europe is blown to the arctic over the drier north Eurasian landmass, so those regions contribute disproportionately more to arctic haze.

Is antarctic haze occurring? Soot and other nongaseous pollution generated in the Northern Hemisphere has little chance of ending up in the antarctic, because it takes as much as a year or so for any constituent of the atmosphere to pass from one hemisphere to the other. The reason is that the prevailing air currents tend to blow air pollution either in an east-west direction or poleward (that is, toward the North Pole in the Northern Hemisphere and toward the South Pole in the Southern Hemisphere). Long before a year is out, most of the soot, trace metals, and acidic pollution generated in the north falls, rains, or snows out of the atmosphere. Moreover, only a small fraction of the world's industrial activity occurs in the Southern Hemisphere. Hence, antarctic haze is not a problem at present.

Previously, some scientists had speculated that the sooty carbon in the arctic air was the product of natural forest fires, rather than industrial combustion. But a clever application of carbon isotope dating ruled out that possibility. Carbon isotope dating works as follows. Cosmic rays are continually creating a rare variety of carbon atom in the atmosphere. This variety, or isotope as atomic physicists call it, has a heavier nucleus than the ordinary type. Unlike the common variety, the atoms of this heavier isotope do not last forever; they decay slowly and turn into nitrogen atoms. On the average, any given atom of the heavy variety will live about eight thousand years before decaying. In the atmosphere, this carbon isotope is found in the gas, carbon dioxide. When green plants take up carbon dioxide in photosynthesis, some of the carbon that they incorporate into their woody tissue will be this rare type. Then, slowly, the rare carbon atoms decay away, eventually leaving only the common type. In the ordinary application of carbon dating, used by archaeologists, the age of the wood can be determined by measuring how much of the rare carbon is left in it.

This method can be used to determine the source of the carbon in arctic haze by noting that when a forest burns and the carbon in the wood is turned to carbon dioxide or carbon soot, some of this carbon will be of the heavy variety. In contrast, when coal or oil or natural gas is burned and the carbon in those fuels is turned to carbon dioxide or carbon soot, there will be practically no heavy carbon atoms present. This might seem surprising, considering that these fossil fuels were originally green plants and therefore once had about the same amount of heavy carbon as do the present-day forests. But the reason the carbon atoms in coal and oil are practically all of the common type is that the rare carbon isotope has gradually decayed away over the millions of years that the fossil fuel has been sitting in the ground. So, we can tell whether the carbon soot in the arctic originated from forest fires or from coal, oil, and natural gas by measuring the amount of the heavy carbon isotope in the soot. When this was done, the very low amount of heavy carbon showed that forest fires were not the source of the soot.

Returning to the Brooks Lake nitrogen budget, we measured the levels of nitric acid in Alaskan precipitation at Katmai National Park and found them to be low compared to the sulfuric acid levels. Nevertheless, since nitric acid contains a fertilizer form of nitrogen, we figured out the contribution of this nitrogen source to the Brooks Lake nitrogen budget. The answer is that roughly ten to twenty tons of nitrogen per year are dumped on the watershed by precipitation, an amount that is about the same as the contribution from nitrogen-fixing lichens, but that is small compared to the turnover of nitrogen within the soil or the lake.

Although arctic haze does not directly affect our nitrogen budget significantly, it poses other, more serious, threats. First, the sooty carbon can alter the climate of the arctic because it absorbs sunlight. This has the effect of warming the arctic, because the sunlight that gets absorbed by the soot would otherwise have simply been reflected off the icy surface and lost to space. Instead, the soot warms up and radiates heat back to the surface. Had there been less ice and snow at the surface, so that it absorbed more sunlight and reflected less, as is the case for most of the earth, then the sooty carbon would have the opposite effect: it would cool the surface of the earth below the polluted air.[7]

To the best of our understanding, the present level of arctic haze is warming large areas of the northern latitudes by 1 to 2°F during the springtime. This may not seem like a very serious problem and

7. The reason is that, while ice and snow absorb heat, they do not absorb sunlight but reflect it. The soot, by absorbing sunlight and radiating it to the surface, creates a heat source that was not there previously. However, for surfaces that absorb sunlight, and thus are warmed by it, the story changes. Now some of the sunlight that would have been absorbed by the surface and directly heated it, is instead absorbed by the soot. While the soot radiates some of this heat back to the surface, the rest gets radiated (and effectively lost) to space. So the surface does not get all the heat from the sunlight that it did previously, and thus the net effect is a cooling. That is why the climate gets temporarily cooler as a result of volcanic eruptions near the equator (like the massive 1883 eruption at Krakatoa in Indonesia) or in the middle latitudes. A nuclear war would also cause the planet to cool because the soot from the fires caused by the detonating bombs would mainly reside in the atmosphere over the midlatitudes, where the major war targets are located. It is only in the shiny polar regions that light-absorbing pollution in the atmosphere brings about a warming rather than a cooling effect.

might even be viewed as a blessing by people living in that cold climate, but, in fact, it could trigger a chain of events with grim worldwide consequences.

If the pollution continues, even at its present level, the slight warming it causes will slowly over time melt vast amounts of snow and ice. If you could view the region from space, you would see it beginning to look darker—less shiny—because the area covered by ice or snow will have shrunk. This will greatly accelerate the warming trend, because more sunlight will be absorbed at the surface. This could warm the arctic and subarctic by far more than one or two degrees and not just in the springtime.[8] A recent study by Peter Wadham at the Scott Polar Research Institute in Cambridge, England, suggests that during the past ten years, arctic ice north of Greenland thinned by about 15 percent over an area of one hundred thousand square miles. Whether this is the result of arctic haze, or an early warning sign of the greenhouse effect, or just a perfectly natural fluctuation in ice thickness cannot be determined without further study. If the trend is real, then a vast reduction in the area of arctic ice—and therefore a great increase in the amount of sunlight absorbed by the arctic surface—can be expected during the coming century.

Because many features of arctic and subarctic ecosystems make them highly vulnerable to an increase in temperature, warmer temperatures will be dramatically disruptive to life there. One of these features is the rich, deep soils of the arctic tundra and the subarctic boreal forests. These soils have accumulated considerable carbon-rich organic matter, because plant growth is amply promoted by the long sunlit summer days, but the cold temperatures retard the rate at which dead plants decompose. A warming of these soils is likely to speed up microbial activity in the soil, leading to the production of carbon dioxide as the rich organic carbon content of these soils decomposes. As we will see in chapter 2, that carbon dioxide will contribute to the warming of the entire planet.

Warmer temperatures could also dry up numerous ephemeral ponds located throughout the tundra that are used by vast numbers of waterfowl for nesting habitat. Several feet under much of the arctic tundra,

8. On the one hand, warming will melt ice, which will darken the surface, which, in turn, will absorb more sunlight and increase the warming. On the other hand, atmospheric haze above a dark surface cools, not warms, as noted in the text. Which of these two competing effects wins out? The former, whose magnitude vastly outweighs the latter.

the soils do not thaw in summer, creating a condition called permafrost. Should permafrost melt as a result of climate warming, the land surface would change and vast depressions would probably form. Presently existing roads across the permafrosted tundra would be unusable. Along the margins of the sea, ice floats are a critical element of the habitat of marine mammals such as walruses and seals, who rely on sea ice for access to areas that are rich in food. As sea ice melts under a warmer climate, feeding grounds may become inaccessible to these creatures. Cold waters contain more oxygen than warm ones, so as the subarctic waters of places like Brooks Lake and its tributaries warm, there may be too little oxygen for the successful egg and hatchling development of fish.

These types of ecological stress are just a few of the many that can be anticipated from a warming of the far north. Their possibility underscores the need to preserve genetic diversity in wild species, for as explained earlier, such diversity is a kind of wealth that bestows resiliency on organisms subjected to unexpected stresses. Ironically, at the same time that humanity is causing an increase in a wide variety of such stresses around the world, we are reducing genetic diversity through a variety of activities that will be discussed later.

The consequences of arctic warming will be felt far beyond the arctic, for such warming will change the global pattern of winds and alter climate throughout the Northern Hemisphere. As arctic and subarctic soils decompose, the global atmosphere will be altered. Moreover, as the water from the melting ice flows to the sea, sea level will gradually rise around the world.

Another reason for concern over arctic haze is that some of its ingredients are known, from evidence in other parts of the world, to poison a variety of organisms. Certain lichens are notoriously sensitive to air pollution, and some scientists have suggested that the microorganisms that fix nitrogen, including those associated with lichens and alders, are highly vulnerable to certain common air pollutants. Short-term experimental exposures of lichens to pollution do not indicate that the current pollution levels in the arctic are causing damage to them. However, quite subtle effects may be occurring which would not show up until the damage is essentially irreversible.

If lichens in the far north were severely damaged by arctic haze, the consequences could be catastrophic. We have seen that lichens contribute to the nitrogen fertilization of some inland and coastal waters. In addition, lichens such as the reindeer moss (not a true moss, despite its name) provide the major part of the diet for caribou in the arctic. Moreover, lichens are adept at soil building, and thus, in areas where existing vegetation and soils have been devastated by volcanic eruptions, lichens are often the first type of organism to colonize the barren ground and prepare the way for grasses, shrubs, and, later, trees.

In 1918, an immense volcanic eruption occurred at Katmai and covered part of what is now the national park with a thick ash layer. The sound of the eruption was heard as far away as Anchorage, four hundred miles to the east, and the material it ejected blackened the skies over much of western Canada.[9] Visibly dramatic evidence of the eruption dominates much of the landscape; throughout several tens of square miles of the park, the ash was deposited in a layer up to one hundred feet deep. To this day, the areas covered by the deepest ash are nearly devoid of life. But at the edges of the devastated area, vegetation is returning as soil is gradually built up by colonizing organisms like the lichens.

Nitrogen-fixing lichens are beautifully designed for this role. They do not require soils that are rich with nitrogen because they can obtain it from the atmosphere. Moreover, the lichen's fungus can readily rot biological matter, thus providing the inorganic phosphorus needed for plants to grow. Lichens can also speed up the weathering or disintegration of rock, yielding nutrients in the process. And whereas most plants usually shrivel up and die from intense and prolonged dryness, many lichens are capable of dehydrated dormancy from which they recover quickly when the rains come. Because of the importance of lichens in arctic ecosystems, their demise could result in major ecological shock waves. Ecologists call organisms that play such a role keystone species because, like the keystone in a building, removal results in far-reaching damage.

9. A curious remnant of this event caught our curiosity. From our campsite on the shore of Naknek Lake at Katmai, we often saw blobs of ocher, mustard, brick red, or gray things bobbing on the water surface. They were pieces of pumice, a porous mineral often ejected in volcanic eruptions. Paul Jokiel of the University of Hawaii has argued that such floating pieces of volcanic pumice out at sea may play a role in the dispersal of marine organisms, and, in particular, pumice from eruptions in the tropics may have rafted coral larvae to the Great Barrier Reef, thereby helping to create the extraordinary biological diversity found there.

The pollution that causes arctic haze originates with the burning of petroleum and coal throughout the Northern Hemisphere, but that is not the only way in which fossil fuel use has affected the Alaskan fisheries and the other biological riches of the far north. Some of the burned oil comes from Alaska, and bringing it south is fraught with danger. A massive oil spill released over ten million gallons of petroleum into Prince William Sound, Alaska, in early spring 1989, when the tanker Exxon *Valdez* went aground in clear weather. The number of birds killed by the petroleum, just within a few months after the accident, was estimated in the hundreds of thousands. Nearly half the sea otters and other sea mammals in the vicinity were killed as well, and the damage to the salmon, herring, cod, and shrimp industries is probably going to add up, in economic terms alone, to hundreds of millions of dollars a year for many years into the future. This represents not only economic and ecological catastrophes but a social one as well. Village life in this part of Alaska is based on fishing and tourism, both of which are dead for now.[10] When the subsistence base of communities is destroyed, the disintegration of the social order begins as well.

In ecological terms, the long-term damage is also inestimable. Because the waters are cold, little of the petroleum will evaporate; because the shoreline is rocky, it is difficult to clean up the gunk that washes ashore. Hence, the petroleum residues in Prince William Sound are going to remain for decades. Moreover, within a month or so after the accident, large quantities of petroleum had washed ashore as far west as the starting point of this story—Katmai National Park. Even the grizzly bears might be harmed as they ingest oil-polluted fish and gradually build up toxic levels of poisonous hydrocarbons in their flesh.

This will not be the first time that humanity's thoughtless actions caused poison to move up the food chain, from small organisms to larger ones, ultimately threatening the large mammals of the arctic. Years of atmospheric nuclear weapons testing by the nuclear powers in the 1950s and 1960s released radioactive cesium, which ended up in the arctic atmosphere, as arctic haze does. When the radioactive atoms

10. To make the point that the consequences of the oil spill were minimal, Exxon proclaimed a year after the accident that there were no serious impacts on the salmon populations of the afflicted region. Exxon's argument was that salmon were observed returning from the sea toward the spawning grounds that next year. As we have seen, however, salmon remain in the sea for about four years before returning to spawn, so those returning salmon were safely far out at sea when the spill occurred and thus were not the cohort that was affected by it. Whether they will have surviving offspring and whether those salmon that were fry at the time of the spill will survive are the real issues.

fell to earth, lichens became contaminated but not at levels high enough to harm these important organisms. However, caribou eat huge quantities of lichen, and while they excrete much of the lichen they eat, they retain most of the radioactive cesium. So the cesium built up to a high level in their bodies. Eskimos eating those caribou concentrated the cesium even further, thereby jeopardizing their health. Fortunately, most nations ceased atmospheric testing of nuclear weapons in the early 1960s (with the exception of China and France and possibly other nations newly acquiring nuclear capabilities), so the levels of this radioactive poison have started to decline.

There have been other harmful examples of biological concentration of poisons (called biomagnification). Widespread use of the pesticide DDT after World War II led to toxic levels of it in eagles, hawks, pelicans, and other birds that feed high on the food chain. Biomagnification of aluminum in acidified waters of the northeastern United States has caused the death of trout, and in the Kesterson Wildlife Refuge in California's San Joaquin Valley, the metal selenium has biomagnified to lethal levels in a variety of ducks and fish. Biomagnification can also lead to great human tragedy. Japanese in the fishing village of Minimata were seriously poisoned by mercury that had been discharged from a nearby chemical factory during the 1970s. The mercury had biomagnified in fish and then in the villagers eating those fish. The result was approximately fifty agonizing human deaths and over one thousand cases of severe and permanent damage to the nervous system.

The cleanup operations launched by Exxon and the U.S. government were rightly criticized as being too little, too late. But this criticism misses the real point, which is that once a spill of that magnitude occurs in waters like those off Alaska, the concept of cleanup has to be questioned. No amount of effort could truly "clean up the oil" that disperses from a major spill, for some of the most hazardous components of petroleum will reside out of sight and reach on the seafloor, within the tissues of organisms, or dissolved in the water; perhaps a phrase like "reduce the accessible oil" is more accurate.

Exxon was also criticized for allowing the accident to happen, but again this misses the real point: such accidents are inevitable. In the ecologically valuable and fragile waters off the southeastern Alaskan coast, oil tanker traffic will lead to ecological disasters like that caused by the Exxon *Valdez*. We fool ourselves if we think that more effective cleanup equipment or better screening procedures to prevent irresponsible captains from commanding tankers will eliminate future spills.

The amount of oil that is potentially available from Alaska is enough to fuel the United States for only one or two years, yet in the process of exploiting this small resource, we commit ourselves to suffering an enormous ecological loss, the effects of which will last decades.

The ultimate irony of the Alaskan oil situation is that energy conservation could save us much more energy than is available from Alaska. Arthur Rosenfeld, a physics professor at the University of California, Berkeley, has estimated that if all of us in the United States used the most effective energy-saving light bulbs now available (which are about three or four times more efficient than conventional light bulbs), we would save the equivalent of the entire oil resource of Alaska in a decade or two. Moreover, we would all be richer because we would not have to pay for the energy that our present light bulbs now waste. Many other ways to save energy exist as well. Highly efficient refrigerators are now available, for example, and U.S. car manufacturers possess the know-how to produce safe cars that use half as much fuel per mile as the average U.S. car produced today. When the public demands these and similar energy-efficient products, our apparent dependence on dangerous energy sources like the Alaskan oil supplies will recede.

Yes, we seem to have wandered far. Some initial queries about nitrogen molecules along the banks of little Hidden Creek have opened up a complex collection of issues. On the hopeful side, we saw that rain and snow do not bring enough nitrogen to the watershed to affect directly the nitrogen balance and that, at least in the short term, the precipitation is not acidic enough to damage the organisms that contribute nitrogen to Brooks Lake.

But, looking within a wider geographic perspective, pollution of the arctic atmosphere warms the climate of the arctic and might thereby cause profound disruptions to its cold-adapted ecosystems. On a still wider scale, polar ice melt due to this warming can influence sea level and climate worldwide, and warmer arctic soils are likely to release gases to the atmosphere that will augment the global warming phenomenon that may already be under way as a result of fossil-fuel burning.

When we travel to a foreign land, first appearances often suggest how little we know the culture; but then, after a few months visit, a sense of familiarity and understanding grows. After an even longer stay, however, this is seen to be an illusion, as more of the rich complexity becomes apparent. With our resolution of the nitrogen budget, life in the Brooks Lake watershed seemed like a perpetual, balanced cycle, within which our initial, confusing encounter with the gory chaos along the banks of Hidden Creek made perfectly good sense. Salmon, bears, lichen, flowing waters, chemical nutrients—all seemed to lead to commercial fishing on a sustainable basis. Simple enough, provided the boundaries of the cycle were drawn wide enough to include everything from the lichen on the slopes high above Brooks Lake to Bristol Bay where the middle-aged salmon put on most of their flesh. But the more complete picture must include consumption of electricity and the coal burning that produces it, automobiles and the oil tankers to fuel them, and many other elements of a world far beyond the boundaries traversed by migrating salmon or nitrogen-enriched runoff seeping down the lichen-covered slopes of Dumpling Mountain.

We have just begun to tell the full story of how the expanding industrial activities of a growing human population far to the south can affect Hidden Creek. And we have merely hinted at the more surprising story of how Hidden Creek connects to our own lives. The alteration of such faraway, seemingly obscure places not only can upset a fishing village economy and cause the price of salmon to rise but can, in fact, weaken the very life-support system of the entire planet. The threads left hanging here and to which we will return—the laughing gas produced by bacteria, genetic wealth, organic matter in the soil, keystone species, glacial ice—are but a few of the many strands that form the green fuse, sustaining our lives and connecting them with those of all the creatures on the planet.

The fuse is now lit. It has been smoldering since humanity learned enough technology to wrest some control over a seemingly capricious wilderness. If the fuse is left to burn, the consequences will destroy us.

2

. . . AND DOWN THE RIVER OF GRASS

On the edge of a brackish lagoon, a half-dozen crows had caucused in a mangrove tree, their attention riveted on a peculiar black and white gull-like bird swimming in lazy circles on the water. The bird, a black skimmer, is distinguished by its unusual beak. With an upper mandible an inch or so shorter than the lower, the skimmer makes a living hang gliding right above the water surface with its lower beak in the water, scooping small fish and crustacea down its gullet. A typical glide of 40, 50, sometimes 100 feet produces a faultless, vanishing crease on the calm water surface.

Lazy circles are not part of the skimmer's normal repertoire and, in fact, accounted for the crows' rapt attention. The bird was sick, and the crows knew it. With a graceful dive, one among the crows soon took the first step in the ensuing half-hour spectacle. Though the crow did not touch the skimmer, which was too sick to fly, the direction of its dive seemed calculated to prod the skimmer to paddle a bit closer to the nearest shoreline. Gradually, and seemingly with well-orchestrated gang tactics, the crows worked the sick bird to shore until it was standing on mud in shallow water.

The crows then began to strike. First, from the air, they poked the skimmer with their claws and then, from the ground, with their beaks, continually preventing their victim from returning to deeper water. Encircled, all the skimmer could do in defense was to thrust its beak at one or another of the marauders. The hysterical screams of the hapless bird contrasted with the eerie silence of the crows, although a reason for that silence was soon apparent.

It took another quarter hour for the crows to kill their prey. Probably the skimmer would have died from its disease in another day or so, but the crows may have wanted the sport and certainly dibs on eating it. But life is tough for crows as well as skimmers. Unnoticed by me until then was a flock of vultures, who had hunkered down on the same mangrove from which the crow attack was launched. At the moment of final dispatch, the vultures floated down from the tree, bustled over to the scene, and quickly broke up the incipient crow feast. Squawking and jibbering, the crows now retreated ten feet away but made no effort to reclaim their booty. The vultures, meanwhile, opened up the dead skimmer's belly and devoured the contents. Only a few scraps remained for the crows after the vultures departed.

In Everglades National Park, events like this are commonplace. The same kind of drama is, of course, going on all around you. Underfoot in your backyard, for example, some ants are probably eyeing an already doomed wasp, while a jay may well seize the prey before the ants can carry it away. Perhaps a microscopic amoeba in a puddle of rainwater is about to gobble down an even smaller bacterium, only to be eaten in turn by a larger amoeba. But the Everglades is unusual in that anyone can see the action unfolding there. The protagonists leap from the pages of natural history books and come alive for millions of park visitors.

The Seminole Indians called the Everglades Pahayokee, or River of Grass. Everglades National Park is located at the mouth of this "river," at the tip of the Florida peninsula. The park contains an abundance and variety of wildlife to be seen nowhere else in the United States. Perhaps most impressive are the large water birds: the anhingas, graceful diving birds of reptilian demeanor, often seen with wings adroop drying in the sun after a meal; the roseate spoonbills, like figments of Dr. Seuss, with beaks adapted to shoveling aquatic life from the shallow waters; the wood storks, with their heavy clublike beak, often seen cruising in squadrons through the layered pinks of sunset; and the limpkins, heard more often than seen, particularly at night when their shrieking cries of "kree-ah, kree-ah" pierce the cold air and remind you that this flat vast land- and waterscape is truly wilderness.

So productive are the soils and waters in the Everglades that over three hundred bird species are supported here, many in sky-filling abundance. Although the mammals, fish, and reptiles are somewhat more elusive than the large wading birds, they are no less exotic; such species as the alligator, the porpoise, the manatee (or sea cow), and the rare Florida panther find their niche in the Everglades ecosystem.[1] The plant communities too—the hardwood forests with dense stands of mahogany and gumbo-limbo, the cypress swamps, the saw grass marshes, and the mangrove margins along the coast—add up to an ecological montage unlike that found anywhere else in the world.

The spectacular profusion of plant and animal life in South Florida is the living part of an intricate ecosystem. Many of the unique qualities of this ecosystem are forged by the geology, hydrology, and climate of the region, which, in turn, are influenced by the very forms of life that these physical conditions make possible. To understand this ecosystem, let us take a broader look at the entire region of South Florida and go back in time many thousands of years, for the park cannot be usefully viewed in isolation from either its history or surroundings.

At some time or another in geologic history, most places on earth were below sea level, and South Florida is certainly no exception. Even in the Colorado Rockies, beneath the floorboards of the cabin where I write, the bedrock was formed from marine limestone deposits laid down hundreds of millions of years ago. The uplift of the continental landmass started 135 million years ago, and it has been dry here in the Rockies ever since. But the drying of South Florida is a different story. Over the relatively recent past several hundred thousand years, South Florida has gone back and forth between being submerged by oceans and being high and dry. The reason is not the uplift and erosion of a continental landmass but, rather, changing sea levels that fluctuate in rhythm with the cycles of glacial activity far to the north. As the glacial ice mass periodically advances southward, more of the sea's waters are locked up in ice, and the sea level drops; as the ice melts, the level rises. During glacial epochs such as the most recent ice age, which ended about fifteen thousand years ago, the sea level was a few hundred feet

1. For convenience, we use the term "Everglades" to denote all the natural vegetation communities in and just north of Everglades National Park. The term "everglades" (small *e*) actually refers to the saw grass marshes only.

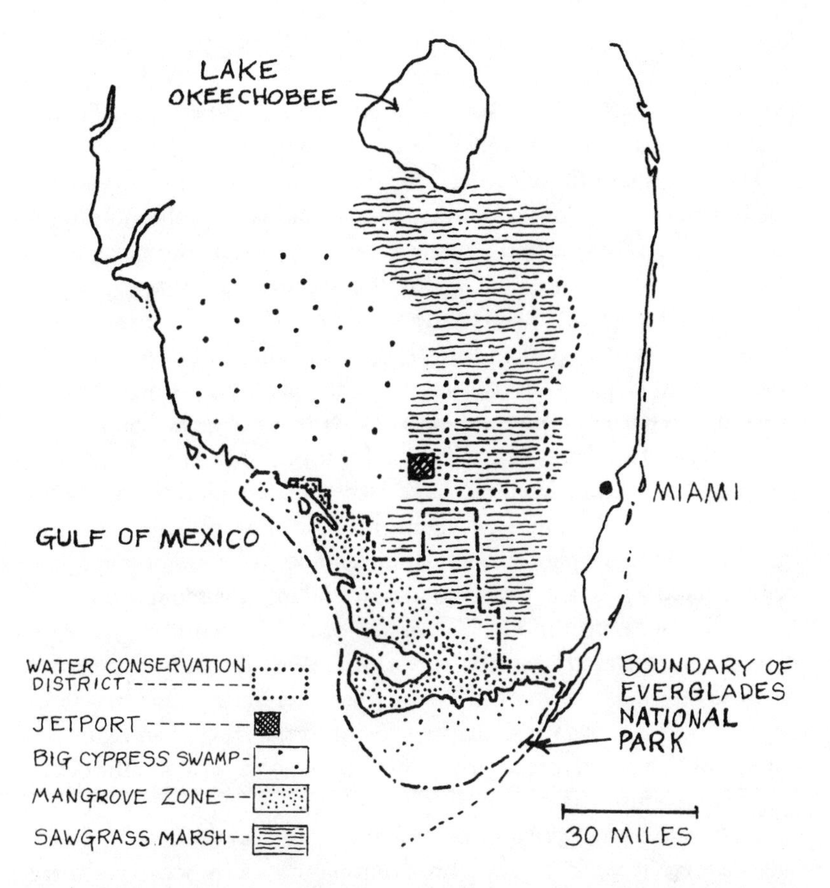

lower than it is today, while in the warmest interglacial periods, it was no more than ten feet above present levels. Hence, in places like South Florida, where the land is flat and only a few feet above sea level, the land area periodically expands due to receding seas and then shrinks as the sea level rises.

In South Florida, only a slight ridge along the east coast, averaging twenty feet above sea level, disturbs the monotonous topography, and on it squats the urban sprawl of greater Miami. The flatness of the region is a product of its geologic history. During those periods in which the sea covered the land, limestone was continuously being deposited on the floor of the sea, thus elevating it beneath and creating the flat landscape. In addition, over the past few thousand years, while sea level was dropping a few inches per century, fresh waters flowing southward from central Florida have deposited on the limestone base the silt they were bearing, further extending the landmass above sea level. This natural process continues today, although its effects are dwarfed, as we shall see, by the influence of Floridians on the balance between dry land and wet land in South Florida and by the influence of all of humanity on the rate of sea level rise.

The same slight tilt of the land that brought the silted waters southward from central Florida still exists today and is of profound importance to the Everglades. This gentle slope, dropping on the average one inch per mile between Lake Okeechobee and the park, supports a surface flow of freshwater down to the southern regions of the park, where the fresh waters merge with the salt waters of the Gulf of Mexico and Florida Bay. That gradual, broad, and shallow flow through the saw grass marshes in and north of the park is the "river of grass." So gradual is the slope of the land that it takes a drop of water many months to complete the journey from the Lake Okeechobee region to the coast.

Of course, many things can happen to that drop of water to divert it from reaching the park. Under natural conditions, it might evaporate, be transpired by a plant, or seep underground into the semiporous rock layers that make up the Florida aquifer, where it then flows through natural underground channels to the sea. With the human presence firmly established in South Florida, the water might also irrigate a farmer's field and absorb some pesticide or fertilizer, cool an industrial engine, flush a toilet, quench a human thirst, or be diverted to the ocean in a flood control channel.

Very little of the water would remain on the land surface in South Florida were it not that something unusual has been occurring there over the millennia. The passage of water downward from the surface into the aquifer is slowed in the everglades by a relatively impermeable layer, called marl, which lies beneath the soil and is believed to have been formed from the calcified remains of decayed algae. Despite the fact that the algal mat grows abundantly along the floor of the everglades marshes, marl formation takes place so slowly that little is actually known about the detailed process. In some areas, the marl is as much as a foot or two thick.

A variety of plant communities exist and compete in the Everglades, their traits influenced to a great extent by the hydrology and geology we have just discussed. The saw grass marsh in the eastern portion comprises the true everglades. Resembling somewhat a Kansas wheat field under several feet of water in the rainy season, the highly productive saw grass marshes are interrupted only by stretches of pine forest and tree islands, or hammocks.[2] Hammocks form either on naturally occurring higher ground where the marl is thicker and higher or on depressions in the seasonally submerged marl, where decayed plant material accumulates around the roots of small plants and becomes peat, thus allowing the transition to larger plants.

Hammocks consist typically of large stands of tropical hardwood trees, such as mahogany, a variety of palms, coral bean, gumbo-limbo, and a number of northern trees, including mulberries, oaks, and maples, growing here at the southern limit of their range. Along the forest floor of the hammocks grow abundant ferns, orchids, ivies, and fruit-bearing shrubs. The pine forests and hammocks provide for wildlife the high ground and protective cover needed for nesting.

Fires have undoubtedly influenced the pattern and growth of hammocks and saw grass in the Everglades since Native Americans inhabited the area. This is vividly described by ecologist Frank Egler:

> In the sawgrass country, the tangled herbaceous vegetation is ready to burn even before the soil is dry, while there may still be a few inches of water on the surface. Assuming that Indians were free and careless with fire, it follows that more often than not the fires would get started at the inception of the dry season in fall. In this manner, the fires would skim over the surface, not damaging the water-covered roots. The fires would smack against a dense hammock and stop, pronto. . . . Then at the end of the dry season, when the peat soil and the hammock trees actually could burn, then there was no sawgrass debris on the surface with which a fire could get started. It is only by this hypothesis that I can logically account for the wall-like abruptness of the hammocks, existing quite paradoxically as dry season-burnable islands in a sea of burned vegetation which sea, without the burning, would quickly be invaded by those same hammock trees.[3]

But the role of fire may be changing. According to Egler, fires occurred frequently and therefore were not intense before white settlement; with the advent of conscious fire prevention, those fires that do occur are conflagrations that threaten the integrity of the hammocks and the saw

2. To convey some impression of the richness of life in the saw grass marshes, we can compare the "primary productivity" of various ecological habitats. This quantity is defined as the amount of plant matter that grows each year on a specified area of the habitat. In the saw grass marshes of the Everglades, it averages about 10 tons (dry weight) per acre. The average value for the earth is 1 or 2 tons per acre, and only estuaries, tropical forests, and highly fertilized and intensively managed farmlands are as productive as these marshes.

3. Frank E. Egler, "Southeast Saline Everglades Vegetation, Florida, and Its Management," *Vegetatio* 3 (1952):213.

grass marshes. Of course, even before people inhabited the Everglades, lightning fires must have had some impact on vegetation patterns in the region.

Across South Florida to the west and just north of the park in inland Collier County is Big Cypress Swamp. Here, several decades ago, grew the most magnificent cypresses in the United States, often so big that three lumberjacks could not reach around the trunk. Now few of these giant trees remain, thanks to a poorly regulated timber industry. Despite this loss, the cypress community is still a vital water source for the River of Grass and is thus an essential component of the larger ecosystem of which the park is a part. In its own right, Big Cypress Swamp is a strange, lovely wilderness, home to a number of rare plants and animals.

Nearer the gulf coast, in the brackish zones where fresh and salt waters meet, the saw grass and cypress communities give way to the mangrove swamps—dense stands of trees interlaced with narrow waterways to form living labyrinths. Mangrove trees grow in the semisaline waters of the estuaries as well as farther out in the shallow waters of the gulf. The red mangrove propagates by dropping into the water seedlings that have already formed a simple root system while growing on the parent. These seedlings then bob around until they reach sufficiently shallow water to form a roothold in the muck. Mangroves also propagate by sending branches down to the muck where they turn into roots and become the support system for the growth of other shoots.

The estuaries are the nurseries of the sea, where many of the ocean's fishes, crustacea, and other forms of life spawn and feed. In particular, the park's estuaries support porpoises, manatees, a large number of game fish (including redfish, barracuda, and various species of trout), and the large Tortugas pink shrimp. The shrimp, of major commercial value in South Florida, breed in these estuaries and are then caught off the Dry Tortugas, west of Key West.

The dense, lush forests of mangrove that line the margins of the sea along many subtropical and tropical estuaries illustrate the high productivity of the estuaries. In fact, the mangrove is as much the cause as the consequence of that high productivity, for the network of mangrove roots and branches below the water level traps organic matter washing to the sea from the land. While trapping nutrients for their own use, mangroves also protect any coral reefs that happen to lie farther offshore from the hazard of too much nutrient.

Just as fire constrains the boundary between saw grass and hammock, so coastal flooding influences the boundary between the mangrove and the saw grass. The rare but enormous hurricanes, occurring roughly once a decade, shape this boundary. The high seas flood back past the mangrove onto the saw grass marshes just inland of the mangrove. While mangroves can tolerate this temporary inundation, saw grass cannot. Between these rare storm events, the saw grass invades the mangroves, only to be pushed back by the next big storm.

During the decades of the 1970s and 1980s, hurricanes were less common and less intense in the southeastern United States. It was beginning to appear that the grand storms of the 1950s and 1960s, like Hurricane Carol in 1953, were things of the past. Over in Africa, in the region immediately south of the Saharan desert called the Sahel, equally unusual climatic conditions prevailed in the 1970s and 1980s, to the extreme dismay of the Sahelians. The region was in the grip of a severe drought. A recent study by William Gray of Colorado State University has revealed a fascinating pattern: from 1940 to the present, severe droughts in the Sahel and periods of lessened hurricane activity in the southeastern United States consistently overlap in time. At this writing, the Sahelian drought appears to be easing, suggesting that we might witness a return of the powerful hurricanes to Florida in the coming years. It is likely that hurricanes in Florida and rain in the Sahel have a common cause and that it is probably related to some feature of oceanic circulation, but what that feature is and why it fluctuates every few decades is not understood at present.

Is it possible that human activities could cause large hurricanes to occur less frequently in the future? The result would be more saw grass, fewer mangroves, and, as a result, declining estuarine productivity. It is, indeed, possible if the ongoing scientific effort to control storms is someday successful. Hurricanes are like wildfires: if you encourage lots of little ones, you may be able to prevent big ones. The hopes of those who would like to litter the Florida coastline with houses rest on the possibility that creating stormlets by seeding clouds will siphon off the energy that can build up to a massive storm.

This effort is misguided because severe storms are essential to the ecological balance and the commercial value of the estuaries of South Florida. The hubris of hurricane prevention is galling. People could choose to live a bit back from the edge of the sea or pay the consequences when their homes are destroyed. But those with the political influence to promote hurricane prevention apparently prefer a more sterile but calm sea to a richly productive and occasionally violent one.

Approximately fifty-five inches of rain fall on South Florida each year, nearly twice the world average. But most of that rain falls between May and October, so there is a distinct dry season in the Everglades in winter and early spring. Wildlife has adapted to this cycle of wet and dry seasons in unusual ways. Seasonally varying rainfall gives rise to variation in the overland flow of freshwater through Collier, Dade, and Monroe counties and into the park. Summer ends, and over the next three months, the everglades slowly dry. In late summer, the saw grass marshes may be submerged under three, four, or even five feet of water; in the late winter, much of that land is dry. How, then, do the animals survive the dry period? The alligator, it seems, is the animal that saves them.

Scattered through the everglades are depressions in the marl, measuring anywhere from ten to one hundred feet in diameter and typically several feet deeper than the surrounding marsh. With tails flailing, alligators scoop out accumulated soil and plant litter from these depressions, seasonally maintaining them against the leveling forces of the water. It is part of the mystery of the everglades, however, that their origin is unknown. Here, in these "alligator holes," scarce water collects and forms pools during the dry season; the underlying marl makes the depressions watertight. As a result, the aquatic and semiaquatic forms of life such as plankton, crustacea, fish, frogs, snakes, turtles, marsh birds, and, of course, alligators have enough water to survive the dry season. Like the lichens that colonize the ashy landscape in the aftermath of a volcanic eruption, these alligators are an example of what ecologists call keystone organisms—ones whose existence makes possible the survival of numerous other plants and animals.

Not only do many species squeak through the dry season because of alligator holes but some even choose this time to reproduce. Animals whose young hatch when the water levels are lowest place the greatest demands on the food supply at this critical time. Like suburbanites watering their lawns during droughts or travelers driving Winnebagos during times of gasoline shortage, these creatures seem oblivious to the constraints imposed by the surrounding environmental stress.

The wood stork, with its clublike beak, is a good example. But as J. J. Audubon's keen observation shows, first impressions can be deceiving, at least for the wood storks:

> This species feeds entirely on fish and aquatic reptiles, of which it destroys an enormous quantity, in fact more than it eats; for if they have been killing fish for half an hour and have gorged themselves, they suffer the rest to lie on the water untouched, when it becomes food for alligators, crows, and vultures

whenever these animals can lay hold of it. To procure its food, the wood [stork] walks through shallow muddy lakes or bayous in numbers. As soon as they have discovered a place abounding in fish, they dance as it were all through it, until the water becomes thick with the mud stirred from the bottom by their feet. The fishes, on rising to the surface, are instantly struck by the beaks of the [storks], and, on being deprived of life, they turn over and so remain. In the course of 10 or 15 minutes, hundreds of fishes, frogs, young alligators, and water snakes cover the surface, and the birds greedily swallow them until they are completely gorged, after which they walk to the nearest margins, place themselves in long rows with their breasts all turned toward the sun, in the manner of pelicans and vultures, and thus remain for an hour or so.[4]

The dry season in the everglades is thus a propitious season for the wood stork to nest; with its food supply concentrated in alligator holes, it can whack to death the large number of prey needed to feed its young.

The Everglades is like a two-cycle engine: in the wet season, there is a tremendous growth of aquatic life, while in the dry season, it concentrates. This cycle of production and concentration of aquatic life then affects the life cycles of the semiaquatic forms of life. The success of these adaptations to the seasonal variation in rainfall depends on adequate amounts of water flowing into the park from the north. The rains cease in September, usually, but the surface flow continues into the early winter and thus shortens the effective dry season from six months to two to four months. Although 80 percent of the park water arrives in the form of rain falling directly on the park and only 20 percent flows into the park from the north, that 20 percent is crucial if the alligator holes are not to dry up. In addition, some moisture in the top layers of peat around the saw grass roots is necessary to protect the peat from the periodic fires, mentioned above, which would otherwise do widespread and long-term damage to the Everglades.

The health of the park is as sensitive to variations in water quality as it is to the quantity and timing of surface water flowing into it, for its animals and plants depend on exceptionally pure water. Even water that is fit for human consumption can be damaging to some organisms, including microscopic forms of life that carry out services like nutrient cycling and thus are essential to the survival of entire ecosystems.

In the everglades, agricultural fertilizers and pesticides and urban and industrial wastes are the prime sources of water pollution. If runoff

4. John James Audubon, *Ornithological Biography, III* (Edinburgh: Adams and Charles Black, 1835).

water carries nutrients from the farmers' fields or from sewage into streams, lakes, or marshes, a bloom of algae is likely to result. Called eutrophication, this exploding biological production occurs in numerous bays, lakes, streams, and wetlands throughout the world.

Nitrogen and phosphorus are the primary nutrients that cause eutrophication. In their natural state, the waters of the everglades would have very low levels of these nutrients—so low that untreated agricultural runoff is generally hundreds of times richer in these nutrients. Even the treated municipal outflow waters from Miami and other population centers in South Florida have levels ten or more times higher than unpolluted everglades waters.

As one would expect, then, eutrophication occurs in the Everglades. Massive algal blooms choke the waterways and fill the alligator holes. As the algae die and rot, oxygen is rapidly consumed and aquatic animals are often asphyxiated. In the marshes between Miami and Lake Okeechobee, nutrient-rich farm runoff has enabled cattails to outcompete saw grass. Unlike saw grass, which sinks to the bottom when it dies, dead cattails form thick masses at the water surface, thereby choking off sunlight to the deeper water, slowing photosynthesis, and eventually causing oxygen levels to plummet in the marsh waters. Moreover, the dense cattail thickets are inhospitable habitat for the storks, ibis, and herons of the everglades. If these overly enriched runoff waters continue to flow into the everglades, there is little hope that the cattail invasion can be stopped before it reaches Everglades National Park.

Pesticides find their way to the everglades because of their heavy use on citrus and vegetable farms and on lawns and home gardens in South Florida. In the Everglades and in Florida Bay, the effects of DDT on the bald eagle and the pelican populations were especially severe during the 1960s before it was banned. DDT levels in brown pelicans were ten or twenty times higher than in fish, while in fish, the levels were thousands of times higher than in the surrounding waters. Here, as in the pollution of the arctic by radioactive cesium, we see the same process at work—biomagnification.

Why does biomagnification occur? A chemical found in an animal's food will tend to build up in the animal's body if the chemical is resistant to being excreted. Only a small fraction of the food eaten by an animal is retained for growth and tissue replacement, while for some chemicals, like DDT, a larger fraction of what is ingested is retained. Usually, such chemicals lodge preferentially in some particular part of the body (for example, DDT lodges in fat). If an animal with a concentrated chemical is, in turn, food for another animal, then the chemical can become even more concentrated in the second animal through the same process. A third animal eating the second can concentrate it still more, and so on. A sequence of animals organized according to who eats whom is called a food chain. The farther up the food chain an animal is and the longer it lives, the more likely it is to have a high level of toxic substances in its tissue.

Bald eagles, white pelicans, peregrine falcons, and other predatory birds that eat substantial amounts of fish were found in the 1960s to be dying out in the United States as a result of reproductive failure brought on by excess DDT in their fatty tissue. Although these predators did not feed on the farmlands where DDT was used, they were at the end of a long food chain, along which DDT biomagnified. Rain runoff carried DDT away from farms to the natural ecosystems where the birds hunted. The Everglades was one of several places where DDT biomagnification caused declines in several bird populations. Now, although DDT is no longer a major concern in the United States, other pesticides still threaten life in the Everglades.

Degradation of the River of Grass is the threat that has attracted the most attention in recent years. Over the past fifty years, the breeding populations of large wading birds there—ibis, wood storks, spoonbills, herons, and egrets—have declined by about 90 percent. This is attributed to a reduction in both quantity and quality of water flowing into the park. Mercury levels have reached unacceptably high values in some areas, probably because natural sources of mercury in the soil are made available when water levels drop and oxygen penetrates the soils. The oxygen triggers reactions with the mercury chemically bound up in the soil, releasing it in a biologically harmful form. A number of nonnative species have infiltrated the everglades (for example, water hyacinths and walking catfish, along with the cattails discussed above) and have replaced native species. Fires, resulting from droughts and water diversion for agriculture and domestic use, have taken a particularly serious toll on wildlife and vegetation in recent years.

In the late 1960s, a new threat to the park surfaced. At that time, one of the hottest environmental debates was over the supersonic transport, or SST, which was designed to carry passengers through the stratosphere faster than the speed of sound. Eventually, U.S. plans for the SST were scuttled for economic and environmental reasons, particularly the threat it posed to the stratospheric ozone layer (although the French-British version, the Concorde, was approved and is in heavily subsidized operation). But in the late 1960s, hopes were high in the United States that the plane would become a reality, and developers in Miami were angling for the chance to make South Florida the port of entry and exit for passengers on SST flights between the United States and Latin America. Because the SST required longer landing strips than those currently available at Miami International, which was already at the limits of its capacity, a new jetport was designed. The Dade County Port Authority proposed that it be located in the Big Cypress Swamp, just north of the Everglades and west of the Water Conservation Areas.

In 1969, I was invited to join a National Academy of Sciences study to assess the impact of that proposed project. Early in the study we realized that the jetport itself, while a source of noise and air pollution, was not the major threat. The real threat was the commercial and residential development that the presence of the jetport would have encouraged. Land values in Big Cypress Swamp were beginning to soar as speculators leaped into action on news of the Port Authority's plans. There was little doubt in my mind at that time that if the plans for the jetport were approved by the U.S. Department of Transportation, then the swamp would be drained. Roads, housing, light industry, and commercial centers would soon stretch across Florida through the swamp. That would be the death knell not only for the swamp but for the national park as well, for the River of Grass would no longer flow to it.

To build homes and commercial centers in wetlands like those in Big Cypress Swamp, the waters must first be drained off the land surface, down to a depth at which, even in years of high rainfall, flooding will not occur. While that obviously destroys the swamp, the damage can in fact be far more extensive. That swamp water is providing human society with a benefit for want of which wars have been fought and whole civilizations have crumbled. It is maintaining the quality of drinking water for people living as far away as the west coast of Florida, in towns like Naples.

How can that be? Swamp water is not terribly appetizing to us. The answer involves aquifers, those same natural limestone formations described earlier that were laid down as seafloor over millions of years. Fresh water is naturally stored within the porous limestone and is available to the large number of South Floridians who drink from wells drilled down to these underground reservoirs.

But a potential problem exists. Since these limestone formations extend well below sea level and out to the present seafloor, what prevents seawater from seeping into the aquifers and salting up the well water? The swamp water above. The pressure it exerts counterbalances the pressure tending to drive seawater into the porous rock. Thus, swamp water protects the aquifers from saltwater intrusion. If the freshwater "head" is drained off the land surface, then salt water intrudes from below into the aquifer. This can be a serious problem: for every vertical foot of swamp water drained down, a forty-foot-thick layer of fresh water will be contaminated by salt water.[5]

This type of salt intrusion is not a threat in most regions of the world, except where people draw well water from low, flat land that is partly or completely surrounded by the sea. Besides South Florida, other places plagued by this problem are Long Island, New York, and many low atolls in the South Pacific.

Salt intrusion had become a problem half a century ago in the eastern part of South Florida: inland drainage for the purpose of establishing agricultural land led to the intrusion of salt water into coastal water supplies. To reverse this potentially calamitous contamination, the counties of central and southern Florida collectively set aside large amounts of land, called Water Conservation Areas. These diked tracts store a modest amount of water above the surface, the main function of which is to serve as a counterweight to seawater, thus protecting the underground supplies. After establishing the Water Conservation Areas and closing off the drainage canals, the east coast aquifer was flushed clean, but the process took many years.

In the 1960s, a similar problem showed up along the west coast of South Florida. As drainage of the western swamps occurred in preparation for tract homes, the first evidence of contamination of west coast underground water supplies by seawater began to appear. As part of the National Academy of Sciences study on impacts of the jetport,

5. Readers with an aptitude for physics may enjoy figuring out where that ratio of 40 to 1 comes from. A hint: the density of seawater is about two and a half percent greater than that of fresh water and 0.025 = 1/40; because of this difference in density, a slightly higher column of fresh water is needed to offset the pressure of a column of seawater. In chapter 6, we discuss how sea level rise from global warming will likely cause salt intrusion into the water supplies of numerous South Pacific islanders.

my colleague Robert Socolow and I decided to look at the problem of salt intrusion in more detail. Using descriptions of the South Florida aquifers, we were able to estimate that draining Big Cypress Swamp would pose a serious risk to available freshwater supplies of hundreds of thousands of people. We argued that there was a kind of symmetry between the east and west halves of South Florida. Just as the humanly constructed Water Conservation Areas protect the aquifers in the east, so Big Cypress Swamp offered natural protection to the western aquifers. We emphasized this in the final report of the study,[6] recommending that the swamp not be drained and, in addition, be protected by the federal government.

The next year or two was a kind of emotional roller coaster ride for all those dedicated to preserving Big Cypress Swamp. The prospects for preservation plummeted shortly after the completion of our study when the discovery of putatively sizable oil deposits in Big Cypress Swamp was announced in the press. Moreover, land prices skyrocketed, as speculators got wind of the possibility that the government might buy out the water rights of the present landowners. Nevertheless, ten years after the study, the U.S. Congress authorized funds for the purchase of water easements on most of Big Cypress Swamp, thus preventing developers from draining the land. It is now Big Cypress National Preserve, thanks to the efforts of the many people, especially the late Rick Sutherland of the Sierra Club Legal Defense Fund, who cared and fought.

The Everglades study left a number of deep impressions on me, including the confidence that scientists can influence public policy when they join forces with people from other disciplines to study the complex issues that often surround social choices. But most important, it made me aware of the confluence of interest between a healthy human society and the well-being of natural ecosystems. Nature, when left to its own devices, provides a wealth of goods and services that benefit humanity. The natural service that we discovered then was that Florida's swamp water prevents salt intrusion into well waters throughout the region. Milton's adage, "They also serve who only stand and wait," applies to the waters of Big Cypress Swamp. In my subsequent scientific sojourns, I have continued to see clear evidence of this confluence of interest between humanity and nature.

6. ***Environmental Problems in South Florida, Part II,*** 1970. Report of the Environmental Study Group of the National Academy of Sciences, Washington, D.C.

Despite the successful outcome of the jetport episode, we worried then that the park might still be doomed. Sewage and fertilizer contamination of the waters flowing into the park were increasing. Rapid human population growth in South Florida suggested that less water would be available to the park in the future. Over two decades ago, Socolow discussed the park's future in a book he and I wrote on environmental issues of the day:

> The odds are that in South Florida the god of unrestricted economic growth will continue to be obeyed, not challenged, until it is much too late. The Everglades Park will be ruined, and one can then drain it and pave it over as well. With the estuaries destroyed, there will be no fishing because there will be no place for the fish to breed. With no aquatic life to worry about, thermal pollution of Biscayne Bay, Florida Bay, and the Gulf becomes less troublesome, and so one could desalinate immense quantities of seawater and service maybe 20 million people living on quarter acre plots across the whole of South Florida. The air would probably not be as bad as in Los Angeles, the traffic might not be as bad as in New York. Man would have subdued the River of Grass and eradicated that most offending of all useless offspring of nature, the swamp. Or, is it just barely possible, there will be another outcome, and our grandchildren will be able to see an anhinga.[7]

In retrospect, Socolow was an optimist. Today, new threats to the park dwarf any of the problems we thought seriously about at that time. It seemed to us then that environmental problems in South Florida were primarily regional issues. You could assemble the local port authority officials, the county supervisors, the mayors, and local conservation groups and hash out all the key issues. That simple vision is no longer believable in the face of the threat of global warming.

By the middle or end of the next century, our planet very likely will be warmer than it has been at any time in human history and just possibly warmer than at any time since the end of the age of the dinosaurs sixty-five million years ago. The projected increase in the average temperature at the surface of the earth is in the range of 4 to 9 degrees Fahrenheit. Now, this may not seem like very much. After all, if you

7. J. Harte and R. Socolow, *Patient Earth* (New York: Holt, Rinehart, and Winston, 1971):201–202. Portions of this chapter, particularly the descriptions of the interaction of water and life in the Everglades and the threats to the park's water, were adapted from material originally written by Socolow and me in *Patient Earth*.

wake up tomorrow to a temperature that is 6 degrees higher than it is today, you might not even notice it unless you keep track of the weather forecasts. But let us place this climate change in perspective. In North America, during the thousands of years that elapsed as we emerged from the last ice age and the glaciers retreated northward, global average temperatures increased by less than twice that amount, in the range of 6 to 12 degrees. So we are talking about a warming that is comparable to that since the last ice age. Moreover, this warming could take place over fifty years, rather than over many thousands of years.[8] The ferocious pace of this climate change will stress life on earth far more than did the relatively glacial pace of warming from the last ice age.

Why is the warming expected? How sure can we be about the predictions? What will be the consequences of that warming to the Everglades, to human society, and, more generally, to life on earth?

The warming is expected because humanity is changing the composition of the atmosphere. Each year we are loading billions of tons of carbon dioxide into the atmosphere. This gas is formed as an inevitable by-product when we burn coal, oil, or natural gas. In the atmosphere, carbon dioxide acts like a blanket, trapping heat and radiating part of it back down to the surface of the earth. We call that process of heat trapping the greenhouse effect. The level of carbon dioxide has increased in the atmosphere by nearly 30 percent since the start of the Industrial Revolution. Roughly two-thirds of this increase is due to fuel burning. The remainder of the carbon dioxide buildup is from the massive deforestation that has occurred during the past two hundred years and continues today as, worldwide, we cut and clear an area nearly the size of the state of Florida each year. Deforestation adds carbon dioxide to the atmosphere because the carbon that constitutes the bulk of a living tree converts to carbon dioxide when the felled tree either rots or is burned.

Carbon dioxide is the most important contributor to the impending warming, but other gases, including nitrous oxide, chlorofluorocarbons, and methane, also contribute. Nitrous oxide is a product of fossil fuel burning and of our excessive use of nitrogen fertilizers in agriculture. Chlorofluorocarbons, a collection of industrial products not found naturally in the atmosphere, not only alter our climate but de-

8. This is not to suggest that the warming following the last ice age was slow and steady. There is accumulating evidence that the warming occurred in fits and starts, at least at some locations, but it is doubtful that a globally averaged change of 6 degrees ever occurred within one 50-year period.

stroy the earth's protective stratospheric ozone layer as well. Methane emanates from rice paddies and cattle feedlots. These gases, like carbon dioxide, are being emitted to the atmosphere at ever-increasing rates as the scale of industrial activity, farming, and grazing on earth continues to grow. These gases are called greenhouse gases because of their ability to trap heat.

Predictions of climate warming must start with estimates of how fast these greenhouse gases will continue to build up in the atmosphere. The rate of buildup is not within the realm of scientific prediction, as it depends greatly on human choices. Climatologists base their predictions of future climate change on up-to-date knowledge of the physical behavior of the atmosphere and the oceans. But they are not good at predicting human behavior, so they do not even try to do so. Instead, they assume various possibilities (or scenarios, as they are called) about the rate of buildup of the gases. For each scenario, a climate prediction is generated using climate models, called general circulation models, that are run on the world's largest and fastest computers.

If we assume that the current rate of growth in population and per capita fossil fuel use continues into the future and that deforestation continues at its current pace, then the greenhouse gases will build up extremely rapidly in the atmosphere. Indeed, about forty years from now humanity will have doubled the atmospheric concentration of carbon dioxide since the start of the Industrial Revolution. Climatologists forecast that in this scenario, we can expect a warming trend of about one degree Fahrenheit per decade. If we could put the lid on the exponential growth of population and per capita fossil fuel use that has characterized the past seventy-five years and only burn as much fuel in each future year as we do this year, then it would delay the carbon dioxide doubling time until roughly the year 2100. In that case, a warming trend of about half a degree per decade is predicted.

Why should we believe these predictions of warming? There are several good reasons. First, the same models used to predict the future can be used to study earth's current climate. While the daily weather forecast cannot always predict accurately whether it will rain tomorrow, climatologists do understand the average properties of our planet's climate. Even before humanity began altering the atmosphere, there were natural greenhouse gases there. Without these gases, the earth would be about fifty degrees cooler than it is today. The models explain quite accurately why it is not so cold on earth. Second, we can use those same models to study climate on other planets. Venus has far more carbon dioxide in its atmosphere than earth; Mars has less. Venus is much hotter than earth, and Mars is cooler. The climate models are able to explain these differences, which result more from differences in the amount of greenhouse gases in their atmospheres than from differences in their distances from the sun.

There are other reasons for having confidence in the models. The climate models tell us that the earth should have warmed up about one degree Fahrenheit during the past one hundred years as a result of the existing increase in atmospheric greenhouse gases. In scientific papers and congressional testimony, climatologists studying this issue have reported that climate data gathered from all over the earth seem to agree with this; the planet warmed up by roughly the expected amount during this time. Moreover, the seven hottest years of this century are reported to have occurred in the decade of the 1980s and the first two years of the 1990s—an unlikely statistical fluke. For all these reasons, there is little doubt in the minds of the overwhelming majority of climatologists and other atmospheric scientists that the earth will warm significantly if fossil fuel burning and deforestation continue.

We have traversed far from the local problems of the Everglades to the globally overshadowing one of greenhouse warming, but before we return, we must go one step further, to the antarctic. From its thick ice shelf, there has emerged one additional piece of evidence that suggests today's climate models may actually be underestimating the magnitude of the impending warming. An international research team recently drilled a long ice core from the antarctic. Called the "Vostok core" after the Russian name for the site of the drilling, the extracted ice contains a record of past climatic and atmospheric conditions. The deeper the ice, the longer ago it was formed; the entire core spans one hundred sixty thousand years, starting with the present. Temperatures during that time interval can be estimated from the amount of a rare form of oxygen[9] found at different depths within the core. The amounts of various gases in the atmosphere at the time a layer of ice was formed can be estimated from trapped bubbles of gas within the ice core because falling snow or rain pick up small amounts of those gases in pro-

9. This rare form of oxygen is the isotope called oxygen-18. It differs from ordinary oxygen in possessing a slightly heavier atom. As a result of the increased "sluggishness" of the heavier atom, water that contains it will evaporate at a slightly lower rate than does water containing ordinary oxygen. Scientists have been able to take advantage of the fact that the difference in rates depends on temperature to reconstruct ancient temperatures from the oxygen-18 record in ancient ice.

portion to their abundance in the atmosphere. The Vostok core shows that over that sweep of time, temperature varied in lockstep with the amounts of carbon dioxide and methane (both greenhouse gases) in the atmosphere. When the climate was warm, the levels of greenhouse gases in the atmosphere were high; during colder times, the levels of those gases were lower. That would seem to be consistent, at least qualitatively, with the notion that greenhouse gases warm the climate.

But things are not that simple. The layers of the core cannot be dated so precisely that we can tell whether the times of peak temperature came before or after the times of peak greenhouse gas levels. In other words, we cannot tell whether the warm temperatures are causing or are caused by the elevated greenhouse gas levels. Either way, however, the message of the Vostok core is profound. According to our present models, the magnitude of the changes in the greenhouse gases in the core is too small to explain the magnitude of the temperature variation. So if the changing greenhouse gas levels were the sole cause of the changing temperatures, our models are too optimistic.

If, however, there were other causes of the one hundred sixty thousand years of climate change, as most climate scientists believe,[10] then changes in climate surely must have caused the changes in the greenhouse gas levels (it would be asking too much to expect the synchronous variation of the two to be a result of chance alone). This would be an example of what scientists call a positive feedback effect—a circular sequence of events in which a change in some component of the cycle triggers causes and effects around the cycle that eventually reinforce the change in the first component. A mechanism to explain how the atmospheric level of carbon dioxide might have increased as a consequence of climate warming can be imagined. Soils contain relatively large stocks of carbon in the form of organic matter; this organic carbon could readily decompose into carbon dioxide fastest during warm periods. Thus, the Vostok data suggest the possibility that climate warming results in more greenhouse gases, and that, of course, will cause additional warming. If this is the case, then the climate models used today to predict the climatic consequences of the current buildup

10. The triggering events that are believed to have caused most of the major variations in the earth's climate over the past million years, including the major ice ages, are changes in the amount and seasonal distribution of sunlight received on earth. The amount and seasonal distribution of sunlight vary over time because of regular changes in the shape of our planet's orbit about the sun and in the tilt and orientation of its polar axis.

of greenhouse gases from human activity are inadequate, for they neglect the additional buildup of these gases that will be triggered by the warming. In that sense, they underestimate the amount of warming that will eventually occur.

To discern the human and ecological implications of greenhouse warming, it is very important to distinguish between what the models can predict with near certainty and what is still speculative. Warmer weather is virtually certain to occur in most locations, with a great increase in the number of days in which searing summer heat waves of over one hundred degrees sweep through our cities. Sea level will rise, probably by as much as two or three feet during the coming century as glacial and polar ice melt and as the sea expands because of its higher temperature. This will cause massive flooding of many populated areas of the world, including, for example, the Everglades and other lowland areas along the coasts of Europe and the United States as well as in some Third World nations such as Bangladesh, where millions of people live and farm within several feet of high tide. The evidence suggests that, already, the seas have risen an inch or two over the past one hundred years, an effect that is consistent with the reported global temperature rise.

Water supplies are also likely to be affected by climate warming. It is likely that tens of millions of people, including many inhabitants of South Florida, will lose their water supplies to saltwater intrusion because of sea level rise. Hotter temperatures and earlier snowmelt will very likely lead to drier summer soils in many parts of the world and thereby greatly reduce world food production.

Unfortunately, the climate models cannot give us reliable forecasts of precisely how much change in rainfall will occur in specific locations. Such information is critical in agriculture, and hence we cannot predict in detail the impacts of climate warming on agricultural production. The heat waves and droughts of the past few years give us a preview of the *kinds* of climate stress that we might expect, but at best they are only a rough guide. Nor can the climate models give us the information necessary to know whether or where to build new water storage facilities to cope with future drought.

Severe impacts of global warming on natural ecosystems, as well as on agriculture, can be anticipated. The biological extinction crisis that the world faces today, brought on by massive deforestation, water diversion and impoundment, urbanization, and pollution, will almost certainly pale in comparison with the devastating impacts in the next century as climate warming alters the habitats of wild plants and animals.

For example, rising sea level will flood our productive and biologically diverse coastal wetlands. Because the land in South Florida is so very low and flat, the projected rise in sea level in the next century will lead to the submergence of roughly one-third of the present area of Everglades National Park. Thus, past efforts to save the park from numerous local threats to its survival are likely to be swamped by rising seas.

It is highly likely that the impending climate warming will be accompanied by changes in the frequency of large hurricanes, which, we saw earlier, affects the ecological integrity of the coastal zone. Whether severe hurricanes will become more or less frequent is not predictable at present.

If global warming causes severe hurricanes to become less frequent, the problem for the everglades is one of not enough flooding. The problem caused by sea level rise is one of too much flooding. At this point, some readers may be tempted to conclude that these two opposing effects will surely cancel each other. Unfortunately, nature does not work that way. Expecting a cancellation of the influence on Everglades ecosystems of these two kinds of sea level change is like expecting a person who fasts for half the days of each month and binges for the other half to remain healthy.

Everglades National Park exists today because of the foresight of many individuals who, over the past decades, have loved the Everglades and fought to save them from destruction. Foremost among them is Marjorie Stoneman Douglas, born in 1891, who wrote the 1947 classic, *The Everglades: River of Grass,* and who still participates in the effort through the Friends of the Everglades, an organization that she founded in 1947. The National Audubon Society, which played a large role in establishing the national park in 1947, has also been actively engaged since then in the fight to save this biologically diverse and lovely wilderness.

Over the years, the nature of the threat to the Everglades has undergone a sinister evolution. Once it was hunters slaughtering egrets for their plumes and alligator poachers satisfying the careless whim of the fashionable for alligator hide. The poaching still goes on today, unfortunately, and threatens the very existence not only of the everglades alligators but of all those organisms whose life cycle we saw intertwine with theirs. More recent threats to the Everglades arise from activity that is not always deliberately malicious but is potentially more devastating because the technological arsenal humanity now employs in bending nature to its convenience is so formidable. The entire park is in the process of being overwhelmed.

Although the fight to save the park is often joined, understandably so, around specific development schemes such as the flood control and agricultural irrigation projects that threaten the park's water supply, or the proposed jetport, the root causes lie deeper in the unrelenting pressure for growth not just in South Florida but worldwide.

When many of today's adults were children, they enjoyed plentiful access to open spaces and can now recall thrilling encounters with wildlife. The landscape possessed a natural integrity, unmarred by tract homes stretching to the horizon; most rivers flowed undammed; most wetlands had not yet been filled in. Memories of that earlier ecological richness are an important part of the motivation for many people who today are joined in the effort to preserve nature.

The education of a new generation is one of the many reasons that the Everglades is so worthy of protection. Half a million kids visit Everglades National Park each year. Many, particularly those from cities, may never have a better chance to witness wilderness and the drama of natural history. What will motivate the adults of tomorrow to fight to save wilderness if, as children, they never have the opportunity to see it? I fear that loss of biodiversity will beget further loss because it deprives children of the knowledge of what they are increasingly missing; it is sure to lead to a sociey that never knows or cares about what it is missing. To the extent, however, that kids grow up able to see such spectacles, there is at least some hope that some of them will want to protect places like the Everglades.

Consider, again, the adaptations of life, geology, hydrology, and climate to one another in the everglades: the algae and the marl, the mangroves and the hurricanes, the hammocks and the fire. Consider the cycles that occur in rhythm with the seasonal rainfall, the intricate interrelationships such as that of stork beak and alligator tail, or of distant ice sheets with subtropical coastal margins, or of atmospheric gases and climate as recorded in antarctic ice. These are all a source of wonder. But as the salt-intrusion and the global-warming science show, these cycles, adaptations, and interrelationships are also an intimation of the catastrophe that will occur if humanity continues to tamper with the natural processes that have forged them.

3

An Island in the Alpine Archipelago

Towering above the dusty plains and deserts of western North America, the crest of the Rocky Mountains snakes from New Mexico to the subarctic wilderness of northern British Columbia. Viewed from a summit of this range on a summer day, the valleys below appear to be covered by a common blanket of forest green. The mountain slopes poking through holes in the blanket resemble in texture the flanks of old workhorses, flecked with patches of snow that seem to offer cool relief to these sleepy beasts. Higher still, a galaxy of sparkling summits stretches to the horizons. From the upper edges of the forest to the summit, each peak is an isolated island in a green sea.

One such island is Galena Mountain in the Colorado Rockies, and it is here that for ten years we watched some slimy, muddy, brown creatures, splotched with faint darker brown, that live in high ponds. Most of a sunny summer day these salamanders just sit on the muddy pond bottom or hover motionless in the water waiting for food to come their way. They sleep all winter. Not much eats them; trout would, but there are no trout in these ponds. If disturbed, they wriggle into the soft mud.

This may not sound like an exciting ten years, but it was. Part of the excitement lies in what these salamanders do not do. Salamanders are amphibians, fascinating creatures that change from water dwellers to land dwellers in their adolescence when they lose their gills and grow lungs. But these particular salamanders generally do not even do that; they keep their gills throughout their lives. Like the dog that did not bark in the Sherlock Holmes story, the salamanders are interesting because they are not doing what salamanders normally do. The main reason we were studying them, however, is that this population of salamanders, like the fuse in an electric circuit box, can warn us when human activities are dangerously stressing the planet.

The presence of nonconforming salamanders was one of several reasons for the Nature Conservancy's purchase of the mountainside on which these ponds lie.[1] The Mexican Cut Preserve, one and a half square miles of spectacular alpine and subalpine habitat on the western slope of the Colorado Rockies, extends from the nearly barren, rocky summit of Galena Mountain, 12,500 feet above sea level, down to a magnificent old-growth fir and spruce forest at 11,000 feet. Within the forest, on a large rocky shelf, sit the salamander ponds, twelve in all, in depressions in the rock that were scoured out by the last retreating glacier. Perched above them is another shelf of glacial origin, with six ponds surrounded by sparse fir and spruce that are stunted by wind, thin soil, and a short growing season. Backed up against this higher shelf is a nearly vertical headwall laced by cascades of falling water in late spring and early summer. That water is the overflow from Galena Lake, the jewel in this natural crown. Above the lake are grassy meadows and steep, jagged avalanche slopes that lead to high ridges and the summit of Galena Mountain.

Eight miles south of the Mexican Cut is the Rocky Mountain Biological Laboratory (RMBL), the foremost biological field station in the world for research and education on high-elevation plant and ani-

1. The Nature Conservancy is among the most effective conservation organizations in the world. It is a private group that buys land on which rare plants and animals live and maintains those lands as preserves. It relies on its more than half-million members for financial support. In the United States, the Nature Conservancy owns over 1,500 preserves, comprising more than five million acres. Conservancy lands are protected against hunting, disturbance to vegetation, and other unauthorized types of activity that could harm the preserves. Numerous endangered plants and animals owe their preservation to this organization. Nevertheless, we shall see in this chapter that preserve status does not necessarily confer protection, for some threats cannot be fenced out. Readers can become members of the Conservancy by writing to the Nature Conservancy, 1835 North Lynn Street, Arlington, VA 22209.

mal populations. Among its many activities, RMBL manages the preserve for the Nature Conservancy and during the 1980s was the base from which my students and I conducted our research at the preserve.[2]

The tiger salamanders[3] at the Mexican Cut are born in the late spring or early summer. Mating and egg laying generally take place as soon as the animals emerge from hibernation during the spring melt; the eggs take about three weeks to mature. By late summer, the young, typically two or three inches long, are not yet developed enough to make the transition from a gilled water animal to a lunged land dweller. Only by the second summer, if they survive the cold winter, will they possibly have that option. By then, they are three to five inches long.

But in the Mexican Cut, over half of the salamanders never undergo that change. They continue to grow, to a maximum length of six or seven inches, and remain gilled water dwellers, called paedomorphs. The reason for this peculiar developmental pattern, shared by a small fraction of salamanders in other locales, is not certain, but it may have to do partly with adaptation to cold climate, for paedomorphs are often found in high-elevation ponds. The pond waters at the Mexican Cut are cold year-round, but for much of the year, the air is colder, so there is an advantage to being able to stay in the water. The more interesting question may be, why are not all the Mexican Cut salamanders paedomorphs? As the salamanders probably have no control over their hormones, this is better phrased as, why are not all the salamanders genetically programmed to this more adaptive life history? The reason probably is that some of the ponds dry up in the late summer or fall, particularly in dry years; those salamanders unfortunate enough to be stuck with gills in a drying pond will not survive. Harsh environments pose difficult choices for organisms.

The choices can be difficult for researchers as well. In summer 1980, I set out with two University of California, Berkeley, students, Dick Schneider and Greg Lockett, to answer for the Mexican Cut the same

2. Over the past 30 years, many important scientific advances were made by RMBL researchers working at the Mexican Cut. Among these is the work of Stan Dodson elucidating the role of body size on the diet of the zooplankton that inhabit ponds and streams. Two RMBL scientists, Robert Willey and Ruth Willey, not only have devoted much effort to understanding the entire Mexican Cut ecosystem but have worked tirelessly over the past decades to secure Nature Conservancy protection for the site.

3. The name "tiger salamander" seems singularly inappropriate for such a drab animal. The name makes more sense when they are seen at a lower elevation, where they tend to be colored a more dramatic yellow and black. They are found throughout the continental United States and exhibit considerable color variation from place to place.

question later answered at Brooks Lake: what, if any, mechanisms keep the nitrogen cycle in balance? We were fascinated by the question of how a mountaintop ecosystem can maintain its nutrients against the losses that occur as rushing waters flush nutrients downhill. To begin, we collected rain samples to measure how much nitrogen is added to the high mountains as nitric acid. To our surprise, the very first rain sample we collected had a level of nitric acid as high as typical rain downwind of the heavily polluted Ohio Valley.[4] We reluctantly decided to drop the nutrient balance project and, instead, study the problem of acid rain in the Colorado Rockies.

The tiger salamander (*Ambystoma tigrinum*) is a close relative of the spotted salamander (*Ambystoma maculatum*), which was eradicated from lakes in the Adirondack Mountains by acid rain. Because different species that are closely related often respond similarly to stresses, the salamanders at the preserve became an early priority for our studies. I began censusing their populations in all the Mexican Cut ponds in 1980, right after our first observations of acid rain. The salamander census has been carried out roughly every two weeks each summer ever since then, with the able help of Gideon Yaffe, Erika Hoffman, Jill and Cheri Holdren, Diana Roth, and Alexis Harte. By the mid-1980s, the unavoidable conclusion from the census data was a distressing one.

We divided the data into two categories: young of the year (those born in the late spring or early summer of the year of the census) and adults (all others). From 1981 to 1987, the adult population steadily declined to about one-third of its original size. Anecdotal accounts of the size of the population in the 1960s and 1970s by other researchers suggested that the total Mexican Cut population had remained fairly steady—around 500 adults—during those decades, so we were probably not simply seeing natural variability in the population.

Our census data also suggested that the decline in adult numbers occurred because of reproductive failure. From 1983 to 1987, our censuses revealed that a total of only about 200 hatchlings were born in the Mexican Cut. Since only a small fraction of these hatchlings survive the first winter, far fewer than 200 new salamanders joined the adult

4. The pH of the storm water was 4.2. The pH scale measures how acidic or basic a solution is. Low pH values correspond to high acidity, with pH 7 being the midpoint between acids and bases. The scale resembles the Richter scale of earthquake strength in that when the pH changes by 1, the acid level changes by a factor of 10. Thus, rain with a pH of 4.2 is 10 times more acidic than rain with a pH of 5.2. Rain with a pH of 4.2 is about as acidic as orange juice.

population during this period of time. Since the adults live about ten years, on average about one-tenth of the adult population should die each year, so out of an initial population of 500, around 200 adults should have died during the years from 1983 through 1987. Hence, the number of adults that died should have greatly exceeded the number of new adults; 200 births over five years is not nearly enough newborns to replace the adults that died naturally during that time. The expected result: a large drop in the adult population, just as was observed. The overriding question for us then became, is the salamander population decline at the Mexican Cut caused by acid rain?

Prior to our 1980 acid rain discovery, neither we nor anyone else had any idea that acid rain was falling on the western slope of the Rockies. Acid rain had been found near Denver and in some areas of California not far downwind of Los Angeles. But it was generally thought that in the western United States, acid rain was only a problem near large sources of urban pollution and not in truly remote wilderness. Maybe our first measurement was a fluke? To find out, we collected samples year after year from practically every rain- and snowstorm and measured their chemical contents.[5] This revealed that the original rain sample from 1980 was about three times as acidic as average summer rain. Pollution levels in rain or snow often vary from storm to storm, and so it is not surprising that our original sample was more polluted than average. Even though the average level of pollution turned out not to be as high as we first feared, it was still polluted enough (about one-third as acidic as rain in the heavily polluted Ohio Valley) to be of concern. We found that winter snow was less acidic than summer rain, mainly because in the high mountains there is far more snow than rain, so the winter acid is more diluted.

If acid rain was harming plants or animals in the Mexican Cut, the harm would probably show up first in the aquatic life. That, at least, has been the experience elsewhere in the world where biological damage from acid rain occurs. And for aquatic life to be harmed, first the chemical properties of the water would have to be altered by the acid

5. Rainstorms sampled at the Mexican Cut and at RMBL showed that the chemistry of the rain at the two sites was virtually identical. Snowstorms were sampled only at RMBL because of the extraordinary difficulty of maintaining a permanent human presence at the isolated Mexican Cut during the winter. Greg Lockett, Dick Schneider, Charles Blanchard, Harvey Michaels, Billy Barr, and Asa Bradman joined me in this phase of the study and in the subsequently discussed work on acid pulses as well.

in the rain. So changes in the acidity of the pond waters are what we looked for next.

Most lakes and ponds are endowed with some natural chemical protection against acid, called acid neutralizing capacity, or ANC. The most widespread example of ANC in waters is dissolved limestone (calcium carbonate, the stuff of seashells). When acid is added to water containing dissolved limestone, the acid is neutralized and so the water is protected. But in the process of neutralizing acid, some of the dissolved limestone is used up. Once the original ANC is all gone, and if no new sources are added to the water, the water will become acidic with the next influx of acid.

Early on we noticed that some of the ponds in the Mexican Cut had relatively large amounts of ANC, while others had very little. One pond had only one-tenth as much ANC as did another that lay only fifty feet away. Was it possible that the ponds once had similar amounts of ANC but that acid rain and snow had removed much of the ANC from some ponds but not others? Not very likely, because the same rain and snow fell on all of them.

The differences lay, we soon discovered, in the types of rock and soil on the slopes above the ponds. Most of the rain and snowmelt that enters a pond or lake falls not directly in the water body but in its watershed, above. The water then drains to the lake or pond either in overland flow, as in streams, or in groundwater flow, which mostly occurs as percolation through soil. The ponds with high ANC had visible chunks of limestone set among the soil and other rocks on the slopes above. As acid storm water flows down these slopes, it comes in contact with the limestone, which neutralizes it, and also brings extra dissolved limestone into the ponds. In the watersheds of the low-ANC ponds, the only visible rock is quartzite, a bluish-white mineral that is a poor neutralizer of acid.

In the Mexican Cut, the ANC of each pond is primarily determined by local soil conditions, which, in turn, are determined by local rocks. In matters of pond water sensitivity to acids, geology is destiny in the Mexican Cut. In fact, this is true in most parts of the world, although there are places, such as large areas of central Asia, where soil conditions are affected more by soil particles brought by the winds than they are by local rocks.

So, some of the ponds were naturally endowed with protection against acid rain. According to the standard scientific lore about acid rain, that meant that we should expect to see the less-endowed ponds turning acid first because they had less ANC to neutralize incoming acid. At this stage, we were quite excited: here was an unusual chance to compare ponds with very different levels of resistance to acids, yet receiving the same amount of acid rain. We had a natural laboratory in which to test ideas about how acid rain damages lakes.

Summer after summer, throughout the 1980s, we measured the ANC of the ponds. No change was occurring in any of them from one summer to the next. The acid rain seemed to be having little effect on the ponds. We did notice, though, that in all ponds the ANC was always lowest earlier in the summer when we first sampled them each year. Was it possible that even earlier each year, perhaps in spring, the waters would be acidic and possibly harmful to life?

To explore that possibility, in late spring 1984, Berkeley student Asa Bradman and I skied the eight miles in from RMBL and sampled the ponds. There was still an ice cover on the ponds, and more than half the winter snowpack still lay on the ground at the Mexican Cut. Just as we suspected, all the ponds had higher levels of acid than we had ever seen in summer. In one pond, the waters along the shoreline were at pH 4.9, comparable to the acid levels in lakes of the Adirondacks and Scandinavia where fish have died as a result. The difference, of course, is that many of the lakes there are now acidic all year long, whereas what we observed was temporary; a few weeks later, the acid levels were considerably lower.

We also noticed that the composition of the acid in the ponds was similar to that in the snowfall measured at RMBL each winter. The clues began falling into place. Late spring is when snowmelt at the Mexican Cut is at its peak, when much of the winter snow accumulation melts in about one month. The melt was preferentially releasing the acid stored in the snowpack first. In fact, about 80 percent of the acid poured out in the first 20 percent of the melt.

This phenomenon of an acid pulse at snowmelt was previously observed in Scandinavian lakes. When acid snow melts, most of the acid-causing chemicals in the snowpack get flushed out in the first part of the melt. For those who live in areas where the county salts the roads in winter to melt ice, this may not seem so strange; salt lowers the melting point of ice, and so do acids. Within the snowpack, acidic snow melts out at colder temperatures than would pure snow, leaving a relatively pure snowpack to melt later when the temperature warms further.

For a while, we had trouble convincing U.S. government acid rain

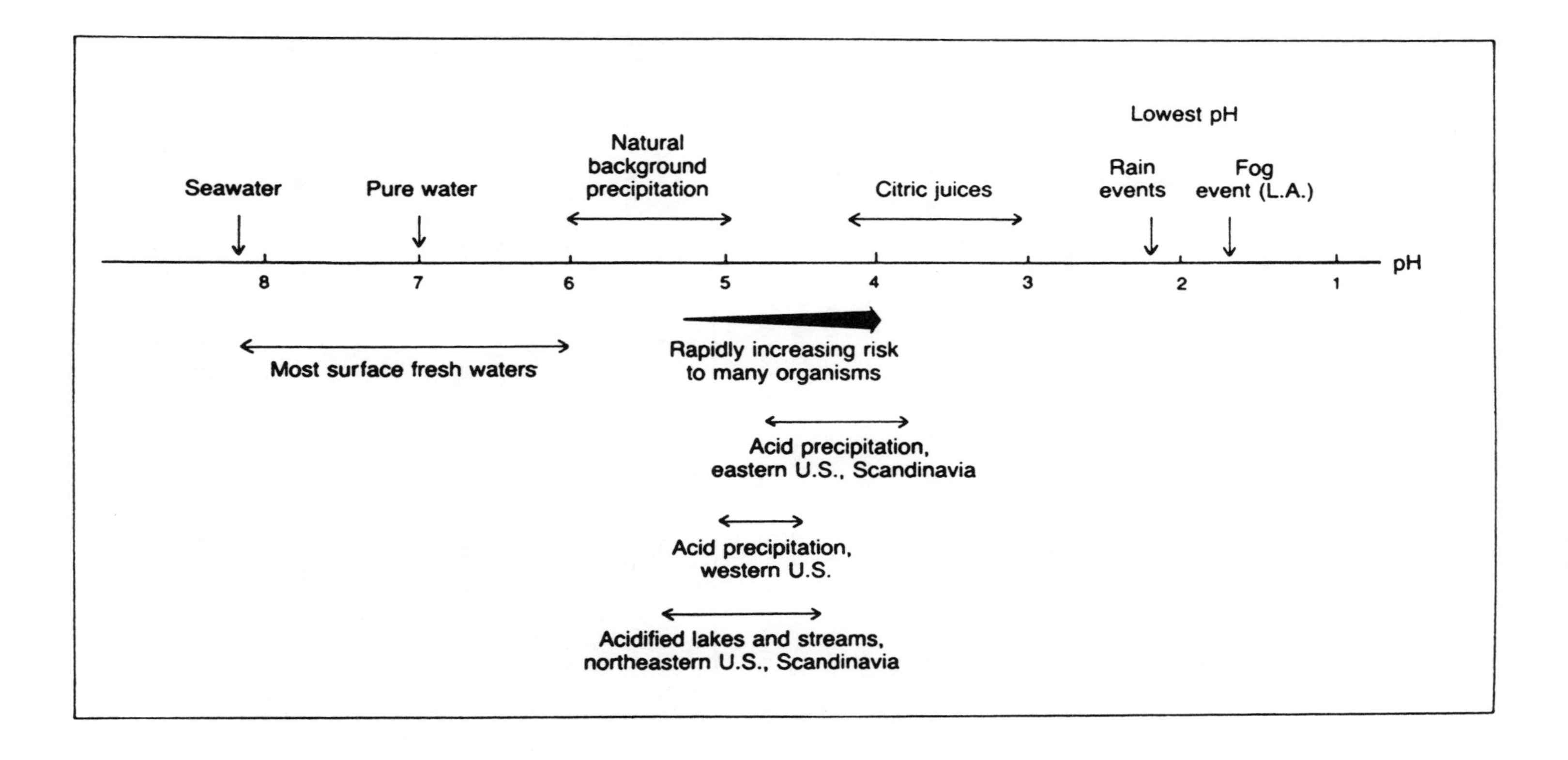
Lowest pH
Seawater
Pure water
Natural background precipitation
Citric juices
Rain events
Fog event (L.A.)
8
7
6
5
4
3
2
1
pH
Most surface fresh waters
Rapidly increasing risk to many organisms
Acid precipitation, eastern U.S., Scandinavia
Acid precipitation, western U.S.
Acidified lakes and streams, northeastern U.S., Scandinavia

researchers that acid pulses were occurring in the western United States. Getting up to the high mountain lakes in spring is somewhat of an ordeal, so some scientists were content to assume that acid levels could not be as high as we asserted. But a few years after we reported our discovery of acid pulses in the Rockies, pulses of this type began to be observed by other scientists in other western alpine lakes and ponds where acid rain and snow occur.

Initially, we were puzzled that the acid levels in the ponds were so similar during snowmelt and so different in midsummer. All the ponds, whether they had high summertime ANC or not, exhibited this acid pulse, which we called episodic acidification. The explanation has to do with the pace of the pulse. The conventional wisdom about ANC affording protection was inapplicable to episodic acidification because the volume of snowmelt pouring into the ponds in spring is so huge that it overwhelms the ANC of the waters. The melting waters literally push out the old water (which had retained the ANC from the previous summer), replacing it with new, more acidic water. The recovery to more normal acid levels occurs soon after, when the rest of the snowmelt comes seeping into the ponds through the soils along the slopes above. This seepage water gets neutralized in the soils and brings to the ponds their summertime ANC. Since the soils differ from one pond to another because of the different types of rocks above the individual ponds, the amounts of ANC brought to the ponds differ.

Although we still did not know in 1984 if any biological harm was caused by the acid rain, one of my graduate students, Charley Blanchard, started wondering where the acidity in the rain and snow at the Mexican Cut was coming from. Back in 1980, when we first observed acid rain there, we had identified three possible sources: coal-fired power plants, such as the ones at Four Corners and at Navajo, Arizona; copper smelters, such as the big one at Douglas, Arizona; and urban pollution, largely from automobiles, which would have to be coming from Los Angeles (since Denver is downwind from the Mexican Cut most of the time and Los Angeles is the largest upwind urban source). Because we observed roughly equal amounts of both nitric acid and sulfuric acid at the Mexican Cut, we were able to rule out some possibilities right away. Automobiles are sources only of nitric, not sulfuric acid, whereas smelters are sources of only sulfuric, not nitric acid. Coal burning produces both. Therefore, it was not just smelters alone or Los Angeles automobiles alone that were polluting the preserve.

There is no foolproof or single, best way to figure out where the air pollution that falls to earth in some remote spot originated. The best strategy is to use many different methods for trying to discover the source and then hope that they all tend to point to the same one. Fortunately, many techniques exist. Weather Service data provide information about the direction of the winds blowing the pollution from source to target. If the winds come out of the southwest (as they tend to do during the most polluted storms on the western slope of the Rockies), then pollution sources to the north can be ruled out. Further information can be deduced from changes in the nature of the acidity. Suppose, for example, that for a few months one year, when the smelters were shut down because of a strike, the normally equal mixture of nitric and sulfuric acid in the rain is replaced by nitric acid alone. That would indicate the smelters were a major contributor to the sulfuric acid component of the acid rain. A third approach is the one that was first used to determine the sources of arctic haze (see chap. 1): trace metal fingerprinting. Polluted air contains such trace elements as lead, copper, manganese, arsenic, zinc, and nickel. Different pollution sources produce different amounts of these, so the collection of trace metals in a rain sample serves as a fingerprint that can be matched to an individual type of polluter.

Using all three techniques, Blanchard was able to deduce that the major source of the acid pollution at the Mexican Cut was coal-fired power plants in the southwestern United States. More than half the total acidity could be attributed to coal burning. The second most important source was copper smelters, located in Arizona and Mexico, and the least important was Los Angeles smog.

To some people, the evidence we had gathered would provide sufficient reason to clean up the major sources of the pollution. But the political process of environmental protection demands a corpse. If no biological harm was resulting from the pulses of acid seen at snowmelt, then many politicians would ask, "Why clean up the sources?" By the mid-1980s, when we had discovered episodic acidification and the declining salamander population, we suspected that these were linked. Yet, we had no real proof. The only sure way to know whether acid in the ponds was killing the salamander eggs was to experimentally subject the eggs to different levels of acidity under controlled conditions and see if egg development was damaged.

In summer 1987, Erika Hoffman and I carried out exactly that experiment. The eggs of amphibia (along with those of trout) are generally more acid sensitive than those of most other animals. But we found the tiger salamander eggs to be sensitive even by amphibian standards. Our experiments revealed that acid levels only a third as strong as those seen in the ponds during the acid pulse were enough to kill half the eggs.

All that remained to clinch the argument was to show that the eggs were present in the ponds during the time of the acid pulse. In 1984, the year we first looked for (and found) the pulse, this was indeed the case. Next spring, the acid pulse was weaker than in 1984, but, again, it overlapped the period that the eggs were developing and could have caused reproductive failure. It was not until 1988 that a dramatic change occurred. In spring of that year, there was no acid pulse, and the acid levels in the ponds never got low enough to seriously impair the eggs. The reason was that the snowpack was thin that winter and snowmelt occurred slowly, so that most of the acidic melt water could seep through soils and become neutralized on its way to the ponds. Moreover, 1988 was also the first year since 1982 when a large number of hatchlings emerged from the eggs (1,500, as opposed to a total of 200 in all the five years prior to this). Here was evidence that when there was an acid pulse, reproduction was impaired, and when there was none, reproduction was successful.

We described our findings in a scientific article that concluded, "Episodic acidification could account for the observed salamander population decline. At this time, however, other causes cannot be ruled out."[6] Why were we so cautious in our conclusion? The possibility still exists that the salamanders breed explosively only every half decade or so and that it was only by chance that they chose to breed in a year with no acid pulse. Ecosystems are so complex that it is usually impossible to make an ironclad case that A causes B. The full measure of this ambiguity must be expressed forthrightly in scientific writing if scientists are to retain credibility.

Nevertheless, when I am asked by a reporter or a politician if the salamander studies warrant action to reduce air pollution in the West, I usually answer as follows: Acid rain is probably damaging the salamander population at the Mexican Cut, but we cannot prove this beyond a shadow of a doubt. Waiting until more evidence is available entails major risks: western salamander populations might be completely wiped out as many were in the northeastern United States, and

6. J. Harte and E. Hoffman, "Possible Effects of Acidic Deposition on a Rocky Mountain Population of the Tiger Salamander *Ambystoma tigrinum*," *Conservation Biology* 3, no. 2 (1989):149–158.

further damage might occur to fish and forests, for example, if the pollution is not reduced. But there are other reasons, as well, to reduce air pollution in the West. Urban smog would decrease, thereby improving human health. Visibility in the national parks and other open spaces of the west would improve. And if pollution is reduced by using fossil fuels more efficiently, the rate of global warming will slow, our dependence on oil from foreign lands or from fragile wilderness areas, such as in Alaska, will be reduced, and the nation's economic health will improve. We already have the technical know-how to greatly reduce fossil fuel use (and therefore to reduce income spent on fossil fuels) by using energy more efficiently. In my judgment, society should take action now to use that knowledge.

To the complaint that it is scientifically irresponsible to venture publicly beyond one's specialized area of research and into the realm of public policy and values, my reply is, "Hogwash. I am certainly as qualified as anyone else to express values and political opinions."

The decline in the population of salamanders at the Mexican Cut appears not to be an isolated phenomenon. Starting in the late 1970s and continuing into the 1980s, researchers around the world began noting that localized populations of frogs, toads, and salamanders were declining. The mountainous cloud forest of the Monteverde Cloud Forest Reserve in Costa Rica is the unique home of the rare golden toad, whose dwindling numbers began to concern scientists in the late 1980s. Similar declines had been observed for other species in Brazil, Canada, Australia, Europe, and the United States. Despite the widespread and heavy use of scientific journals, telephones, fax machines, and computer mail for communication in science today, however, it was not until summer 1989, at a scientific meeting of reptile and amphibian specialists, that these observations were shared and the existence of a widespread pattern became apparent.

Although the magnitude and extent of the declines in amphibian populations took researchers by surprise, in retrospect, it is understandable that amphibia might be especially sensitive to environmental stresses. Amphibia have thin skins that cause them to be extremely vulnerable to dehydration. Those same thin skins leak in the other direction as well, readily permitting environmental contaminants, either in the air or water, to enter. The eggs of amphibia are also very permeable to pollution because they lack the membranes that protect the eggs of most higher vertebrates.

In winter 1990, the National Academy of Sciences convened a special workshop to discuss the problem of dwindling amphibian populations and to attempt to identify the cause or causes. Organized by David Wake, a biologist at the University of California, Berkeley, it brought together specialists from around the world. The workshop produced four major conclusions:

- There is compelling evidence that amphibian populations are declining in many locations around the world.
- The causes of these declines are, for the most part, not identified, although in a few locations, acid rain or some other type of habitat destruction appears to be the likely cause.
- Amphibia, being particularly sensitive to their environment, are good early-warning indicators of environmental stress.
- Since amphibian declines are probably harbingers of further ecological damage, far more effort should be devoted to understanding the causes of the declines and to monitoring the health of other amphibian populations.

I was pleased that the work Hoffman and I carried out at the Mexican Cut, in which censusing of amphibian populations was combined with careful monitoring of environmental stresses (in our case, acid levels) and with studies of the sensitivity of the eggs to different levels of stress, was held up at the workshop as an example of the type of investigation needed to further our understanding of causes.

In locations such as Costa Rica and Brazil, where fossil fuel use is relatively light compared to Europe and the United States, acid rain was dismissed as a likely cause of amphibian declines. Even in such places, however, it is possible that acid rain from other sources is responsible. In Costa Rica, for example, natural volcanic sources of acidity are plentiful. Just upwind of the Monteverde reserve sit two large volcanoes. From one of these, Volcán de Poás, sulfur emissions have recently increased dramatically as the water in its crater boiled away, exposing a liquid sulfur lake. From this crater, emissions of acid-forming sulfur dioxide are two or three times that of a typical large coal-fired electric generating plant. In Brazil, a different source of acid may exist. When large areas of forest are burned to clear land for agriculture, as happens every year during the dry season in the Amazon, the sky darkens for days from the smoke. The first rains that follow clean the sky and may bring smoky acids to the surface waters. In parts of Africa, acid rain has been observed following extensive burning of vegetation, but little data exist to document the importance of this in the Amazon.

Another possible explanation for the decline of the golden toad at Monteverde is the recurring phenomenon of El Niño, characterized by intense drought in some parts of the world and torrential storms in others. It has been speculated that the 1987 drought in Central America, caused by El Niño, may have dried up the breeding areas of this animal.

Returning to the Mexican Cut, one last question about acid rain plagued us after our other studies were completed. The Mexican Cut ponds are only episodically acid; in midsummer, the acid levels in the ponds are harmlessly low. Yet many of the ponds, and Galena Lake as well, have very low acid-neutralizing capacity. If acid precipitation continues, summertime acid levels might increase to the point where life is threatened throughout the summer as well as at snowmelt. Summertime acid levels are low because runoff water seeping through soils on the slopes above the ponds is neutralized by reactions with soil.[7] The ability of soil to perform this neutralizing role could decline year after year, however, unless the soil chemicals that perform the role are replenished. There is a process, albeit a slow one, that does this. It is called weathering, a term applied both to the processes that turn rocks into soil over millennia and to the processes that replenish over shorter periods the ability of soils to neutralize acids. If the weathering rate is too slow to balance the rate at which acid rain strips the soil of this neutralizing capacity, then the pond or lake into which the soil runoff feeds will gradually turn more acidic. Lakes with low ANC are most likely to meet this fate first, and, in fact, this is just what happened to thousands of low-ANC lakes in eastern North America and Europe.

Could this happen to the low-ANC ponds of the Mexican Cut, perhaps in ten or twenty years? How can we predict the future acidity of a water body? The question has broad implications, for throughout the United States and Europe, the number of low-ANC lakes that have

7. In watersheds that do not contain limestone, the dominant process by which soils neutralize acid runoff works as follows. Acid water is acid because it contains hydrogen ions—the positively charged centers of hydrogen atoms. Soil particles also contain positively charged ions on their surfaces, but most of these particles are ions of calcium, potassium, sodium, and magnesium. Such ions are called base ions because they tend to form bases, rather than acids, in water. When acid water flows past such particles, an exchange occurs, with the hydrogen ions from the water sticking to the soil and the water receiving the base ions in return.

not yet become acidic, and yet are located in regions receiving acid rain, far exceeds the number (several thousand) of lakes that have already acidified. In the late 1980s, another of my Berkeley graduate students, Jim Kirchner, took on the challenge of developing a way to predict the fate of lakes receiving acid rain. Kirchner's approach was quite elegant,[8] but to see why, it is necessary to make a short digression and describe how scientists use, and misuse, models for purposes of prediction.

To predict how the chemistry of a lake, or how any other phenomenon, will change in the future, you need two things: an understanding of the processes that govern the behavior of the system and a way of projecting that understanding into the future—a way of "speeding up the movie" so that you can see the future before it sees you. Scientists have found that the best way to speed up the movie is to construct a mathematical model, because such models can be run forward (or backward) in time with ease.

It is easy to make models that predict. The difficult thing is to make models that others can trust. Some models resemble a Rube Goldberg device, encumbered with numerous specialized contraptions and nearly as complicated as the phenomena they try to describe. For example, several years ago, a large team of researchers constructed a mathematical model to explain the reasons that some lakes acidify faster than others. The model required knowing hundreds of quantities, many of which could not practically be measured. So the modelers adjusted the values of these to force the model to describe existing patterns of lake chemistry. But with so many "knobs" to turn, practically any behavior could be accommodated. Some critics have sarcastically noted that the variables could just as well be adjusted so that the model would describe the past ten years of the Dow Jones stock average and then used to predict its future. The point is that if a model does not pass the test of unambiguously explaining (rather than being forced into consistency with) the record of the past, then there is no reason to trust its forecasts.[9]

Kirchner first identified and figured out how to measure the crucial

8. Elegant? To describe a scientific study? Scientists use that word sparingly, but they do use it, usually to describe someone's work when it is lean and graceful, when it makes the complex seem simple, the inscrutable seem familiar. The notion of "fancy" that the word connotes is not apt.

9. Several years ago, I wrote a book entitled *Consider a Spherical Cow: A Course in Environmental Problem Solving* (Mill Valley, Calif.: University Science Books, 1988). Its purpose is to teach people how to make simple yet believable models of complex environmental situations.

chemical processes in soil that determine the amount of ANC flowing into a lake each year. He then selected a dozen lakes in the United States and Canada ranging greatly in size. Based only on a few easily measured chemical properties of soil samples from the slopes above each lake and on the acidity of the rain and snow falling at each site, and using relatively simple mathematical expressions to describe the soil processes, Kirchner was able to predict unambiguously and accurately the current acid level of each lake. That, in itself, is not very impressive, because it is far easier just to measure the acidity of each lake directly from water samples. But by showing that the model correctly predicted water chemistry from soil properties, he then had confidence that he had identified the major processes governing acid levels in lakes.

Next, Kirchner used the same model to calculate the historic changes in lake acidity over the past decades due to acid rain. In most lakes, this record is not known because people were not measuring changes in acidity during the period that many lakes became acidic earlier this century. Fortunately, at the lakes he selected in Ontario, Canada, such information had been measured by Canadian scientists. Kirchner's calculated historic changes agreed with their measurements, thus showing that the model could explain both current acid levels and past trends in acidity. With that, the model was ready to be used with confidence to predict future changes in the acid level of other lakes.

Among the satisfactions that come from scientific investigation is the occasional discovery that many different things are bound by a common thread. In physics, the term "law" is used to describe the central predictions of physical theories, like Einstein's relativity, for which there is strong reason to believe that they hold everywhere in the universe. This is less often the case in ecology and the environmental sciences, where attention is likely to be focused on those things that are unique, rather than universal, about a species or a lake or a forest. Yet, at the same time, if one is trying to develop a way to predict how lakes everywhere will respond to acid rain, it would be costly in time and money to have to build a distinctly different model for each lake of concern. Ideally, different combinations of assumptions would not have to be jury-rigged together to describe different lakes; rather, a single predictive model would suffice. Kirchner's work achieved that. He was able to show that a single master equation described remarkably well the levels of ANC in different lakes and could predict how they respond to future levels of acid rain. Give him some representative soil samples from the catchment area above a lake, and he can tell you about the lake's present resistance to acid rain; give him an estimate of future levels of acid in the rain, and he can give you the first believable predictions for how the lake's chemistry will change in response. He will not have to first ask where the lake is, how deep it is, what plants grow in its catchment, or any of the myriad other questions that explore the lake's individuality. In environmental science, that is elegant.

Kirchner's predictions for the Mexican Cut are somewhat encouraging. If the acidity of precipitation does not get any worse, then the Mexican Cut ponds are not likely to lose their ANC and become acidic year-round over the coming decades. They will, of course, continue to suffer the acid pulse effect at snowmelt time, and that is harmful enough. But the midsummer acid levels in the ponds should not increase detectably. If, however, rain and snow become more than twice as acidic as they currently are in Colorado, let us say because of an increase in the use of western coal to generate electricity, then midsummer lake acid levels will increase and the low-ANC ponds and lakes in the area could become acidic year around. In areas of the world where rain is already more acidic than at the Mexican Cut, Kirchner's work has serious implications. First, he predicts that many low-ANC lakes not yet acidified will become so if current levels of acid rain continue; in other words, we have not seen the worst of the problem. Second, his model indicates that once lakes become acidic year-round, their recovery if and when the acid pollution declines will be far slower than the onset of damage in the first place. In other words, the damage to soil and lake chemistry from acid rain is not as easily reversed as hitherto believed.

There has been a progression of threats to the Mexican Cut over the past century. Some are of local origin, such as miners pickaxing the landscape and cutting trees for lumber, ranchers shooing their sheep up there to graze, and baitmongers catching salamanders for fishermen. When the Nature Conservancy acquired the Mexican Cut, many breathed a sigh of relief; by regulating human activities at the site, the salamanders would be protected from such local threats. But then came our discovery of acid rain, a pollutant that shows no respect for legal land boundaries. As bitter experience has shown at many other "protected" parks and refuges elsewhere, including the Everglades, merely buying land and regulating uses of it do not guarantee the protection of its wild inhabitants. It takes national legislation and even multinational agreements to ease a problem on the scale of the acid rain threat.

But even acid rain may not be the severest or most unmanageable of the threats to the salamanders. Nearly half of the ponds they inhabit are ephemeral, meaning that in some years they dry up because of evaporation. These are the shallowest ones, of course, often no more than a foot or two deep. They dry up in the fall when the previous winter's snowfall was low and melted early in the spring and when the summer was hot and dry. While much of the aquatic life in these dried ponds dies, it is naturally restocked in the coming spring or summer when waters from the permanent ponds, overflowing with snowmelt, flow into the dried ones through the many rivulets connecting them. In all the ponds, however, the water level drops considerably in the late summer and fall. For example, the largest and deepest of the ponds, with an average depth of about seven feet, loses about one-third of its water in a very hot, dry year. Were all the ponds to dry up in some years, entire populations of pond organisms, including the salamanders, would perish.

What could possibly cause all the ponds to dry up occasionally? That is, what could cause snow to melt a month or two earlier in the spring and increase evaporation rates in the summer and fall? The answer, sadly, is the impending global warming caused by the buildup of greenhouse gases in the atmosphere. Global warming will almost certainly negate all the past efforts to protect the Mexican Cut.

This scenario is not confined to the Mexican Cut, of course. Around the world there are tens, possibly hundreds, of thousands of ponds that will dry up for at least part of the year in a climate like that predicted for the next century if current trends in fossil fuel use continue. The loss of plants and animals that will accompany this drying up is inestimable. The populations of water-dwelling life in the ponds will certainly disappear, but the problem goes well beyond that. At breeding time, the Northern Hemisphere's populations of ducks, geese, swans, and other waterfowl are highly dependent for their food on life in shallow ponds throughout Alaska and the northern plains of the United States, Siberia, Lapland, and the western provinces of Canada. While we cannot predict just how many of these ponds will dry up in the coming decades because of global warming, the number will probably be substantial.

The threats to nature from climate warming go well beyond the drying of ponds. Some scientists have argued that mountaintop ecosystems like the Mexican Cut are likely to be among the places where a host of damaging effects of climate warming on plants and animals will first be seen. The argument goes as follows. Suppose you are an insect living near the bottom or on the side of a mountain and perfectly happy with the climate there. If, as projected, the climate gradually warms over the next hundred or so years, you may be able to move steadily uphill and thereby keep within a suitable climate. The reason, as all mountain climbers know, is that it gets colder as you go uphill. A simple calculation[10] shows that it would require climbing roughly ten yards higher each year for roughly the next hundred years to maintain an accustomed climate. Sounds simple enough, even for an insect. But suppose you are already habituated to a mountaintop climate. In that case, you cannot escape the encroaching heat. For that reason, Professor Pete Brussard of the University of Nevada suggested several years ago that researchers begin censusing mountaintop populations of butterflies, birds, and other organisms so that if losses occur, we can detect them. The first fuse to pop on the global circuit board because of the greenhouse effect may well be some little-known organism on a mountaintop.

But even life in the dales is likely to be at greater risk than this argument would suggest, for the slow march uphill will not be an easy one. Although flying insects and birds are certainly mobile enough to move the requisite distance uphill (or poleward three to six miles each year for a hundred or so years, by which means it is also theoretically possible to keep cool), it is not at all clear that plants can do so. And if the plants cannot move to a more favorable climate, then animals may not survive either, because of their dependence on plants for food and shelter.

One reason plants might not simply move to more favorable climates is that temperature alone does not control where plants live. Rainfall, for example, is also very important. The temperature may be more favorable for the plants uphill, or poleward, but if precipitation is too light or heavy or too early or late, then the plant is stuck. Under global warming, the right combinations of temperature and moisture may not occur anywhere for certain populations of plants. Soil conditions are

10. On average, the temperature drops about 1°F for every one hundred yards you ascend vertically. So if the temperature warms at the rate of about one-twentieth to one-tenth of a degree per year (as climate models predict will happen during the coming decades at the current rate of increase in atmospheric carbon dioxide), organisms "simply" need to march uphill about five or ten vertical yards each year.

also critical to plant life. A look at the composition of the soil at the uphill or northward edge of a spruce forest often reveals an abrupt transition in soil chemistry or soil depth. Seeds of any species dropping into the soils beyond the edge of the current boundary of that species may simply not have an adequate chance of taking root.

The reader may wonder at this point how any plants have managed to survive on earth. After all, there have been major changes in climate over geologic history. Plants have survived because they have been able to move in pace with slowly changing climates. For example, pollen from spruce trees dating back to the last glacial period, fifteen thousand years ago, has been found farther south than where that same species of spruce now lives. Moreover, as the glacial ice mass retreated northward, the spruce followed hard on its heels, not everywhere but at just those places where precipitation and temperature were in the range that the species demands. This was possible because the climate change then was at a snail's pace compared to the impending global warming—roughly ten to a hundred times slower as measured by change in degrees in a typical year. Under the slow pace of glacial retreat, soils that spruce could live in had time to form. And there was time for seeds to find regions where there existed the whole complex of physical and chemical factors necessary for spruce.

Man-made barriers may also impede the relocation efforts of wild creatures. For example, the poleward movement of tropical plants and animals may be blocked by a vast tract of deforested land used for agriculture. Birds, of course, could fly over such barriers, but most organisms would not be able to.

The name "Colorado" evokes images of tall mountain peaks, yet most of the state consists of the high plains from which the Rockies rise. The demand for water in those mile-high plains is enormous, for you cannot graze cattle, grow crops, and settle a rapidly growing human population in semiarid regions without it. To get their water, ranchers, farmers, and suburban developers have historically turned to the wettest part of the Rockies, the mountains on the western slope. There, on just 4 percent of the land area of the state, the high slopes, over half of its water supply originates.

If you soared over the western slope of the Rockies in April, May, or early June, you would detect a marked change in the appearance of the landscape above an elevation of roughly 9,000 feet. It would be white, in contrast to the greens and browns below that elevation. In the "high country," as its inhabitants affectionately call it, snow melts late, and there is lots of it. Long after the plains have lost what high-country folks would call a mere dusting of winter snow and entered the long, parched April-to-November season characteristic of most of the western United States, the huge snowpack on the western peaks sits and waits. In late spring, finally, torrents of water pour down the slopes. From the Mexican Cut, for example, the melting snows in June typically release the equivalent of two feet of rainwater falling on the catchment over a period of a mere week or two. The streams and rivers of the high country crest at that time, and the reservoirs and underground aquifers far downstream fill.[11]

In many places, two feet of rainfall in a period of a week or two would cause havoc. Rivers would overflow their banks, soils would erode, houses would be washed away. But without human interference, the mountains can handle this deluge. The rocky banks of stream channels are sturdy, the willows and other vegetation along the shores are adapted to the surging flows, and the soils on the slopes above stay put, bound by the roots of aspen, spruce, and fir. Wetlands in the high mountain meadows along the streambanks fill with the cresting waters, providing habitat for beavers and waterfowl. And the free-flowing, unsilted streams support a bounty of fish. To me, the beauty and integrity of it all is heartwrenching. More practically speaking, the cost of engineering such an effective and biologically productive deluge-handling system would be incalculably large; it could not be built. Yet nature does it all for us—for free.

Perhaps not quite "for free," however, for nature does require one thing from us in return for these gifts: restraint. If the human impulse to dam the rivers, hack down the forests, blast out the mountains and scour the rivers for metal ores, drain the wetlands, and pollute the rain

11. At least that is how it works now. Global warming is virtually certain to lead to decreased snowfall and earlier snowmelt, both of which mean a longer, drier summer. Some climate models predict more winter rainfall in the impending greenhouse climate, but winter rain is of less value than snow because winter rain runoff occurs long before farmers can use it for spring and summer irrigation. One compensatory option for farmers in a greenhouse climate may be to plant their crops earlier in the year so they can avoid the need for irrigation water late in the summer. In regions where, currently, sunlight is ample for crop growth well before temperatures are warm enough for germination, conditions may be suitable for earlier sowing and earlier harvest in a warmer climate.

and snow is given free rein in the western mountains, then our children and all future generations as well will not be blessed with these gifts. Nevertheless, such restraint is not forthcoming:

- Pressure is now building to dam more rivers on the western slope of the Rockies. The claim is made by developers that more water is needed for a growing population on the other side of the Continental Divide in the suburbs of Denver. In 1990, Front Range developers put forth a master plan that included taking water from two streams on the western slope, Copper Creek and the East River, whose confluence is at RMBL. These two diversions, a small component of a much larger project, would have completely destroyed the laboratory's research and teaching programs. At this time, it appears that this particular grab for water has been stopped, but another attempt will undoubtedly be made. The larger problem is that Colorado water law (and that of other western states as well) currently permits water to be taken from one region of the state and shipped to another if lawyers for developers in the latter region can demonstrate a "higher need" for the water. Historically, this has meant that ecological, recreational, and aesthetic benefits of stream water do not count much compared to municipal uses. This ability to destroy one region to permit growth in another is legalized theft; it is equivalent to what in the olden days only pillaging victors in war could accomplish.

- The U.S. Forest Service has proposed clear-cutting forested slopes in the Colorado high country on the inadequately tested theory that this will reduce water loss by eliminating transpiration from trees. In the short term, this may increase water yields in some watersheds. But over the long term, soil erosion from the deforested slopes will clog our streams, rivers, and reservoirs and thereby reduce the water supply for people. Those trees standing on the hillsides perform a valuable ecological service by holding the soil in place; the price they charge in transpired water is cheap indeed. And, besides, the water transpired from the western slope does fall as rain somewhere else.

- The Rockies are already scarred from mining, and numerous streams are heavily polluted as a result. But the worst may be still to come. In the early 1980s, the AMAX Corporation proposed to scoop away the top of Mount Emmons, a mountain adjacent to the town of Crested Butte, Colorado, and eight miles from RMBL. The mountain contained molybdenum ore, the price of which was relatively high at the time. Molybdenum is used to harden steel. Arguing that our exports of the ore to Japan and other nations would not really represent a permanent loss of the metal since it would come back to us in the form of hardened nose cones of reentering missiles, W. Mitchell, who was then mayor of Crested Butte, led a heroic effort to stop the pillage of the mountain. His concern was not only over the environmental damage to the mountain but over the social and economic damage that his town would incur from the boom-bust cycle that the corporation's plans would trigger. The opposition of much of the townspeople and of environmental groups across the nation helped delay the project, and a subsequent drop in the price of molybdenum finally caused its cancellation. But the more general threat from mining operations remains. While the prices of metals are currently sufficiently low to forestall new large-scale mining ventures, only that ephemeral market force stands between mining conglomerates and the fragile slopes.

In a material sense, the consequences of unchecked exploitation of the high country will backfire, for the western economy would be hurt badly if the gift of nature's life support system is shattered. No less important, the degradation of the Rockies would be an unspeakable crime against future generations of people who might someday want to enjoy the beauty of these high mountain ecosystems.

4

Sage Hill: Chaos and Continuity

My mathematical friends would call the gnarly knob of Sage Hill a strange attractor. It is a description my poetic friends would find equally apt.

To a mathematician, a strange attractor is a source of chaos, a place from which numerous unpredictable paths diverge. Descending from the Sage Hill summit through the thick and misty woods, I would start out convinced I was heading down toward my lean-to, only to find myself eventually at the base of the wrong side of the mountain. Small navigational errors, forced by a tangle of fallen beech, maple, oak, birch, hemlock, and pine, added up to one result: a seven-mile semicircular walk back home.

I spent many summers as a kid at Sage Hill in the Green Mountains of southern Vermont, along with thirty or forty other boys from the city. We were under the watchful eye of Mr. Smith, who came out of California, where he had been a forest ranger during the depression, and bought the south side of Sage Hill in the late 1930s. He was in his late seventies, savvy and crotchety, when I was ten and first came to Sage Hill. He ran the camp for six more years—just he and the kids, with no grown-up help—until he had to sell the land in 1955 because of the growing burden of old age and diminishing interest in the camp by a newer generation of television-reared children.

He called it a camp, but it was like no other. We worked much of the day—building the lean-to shelters we lived in, keeping trails clear, cutting firewood, repairing stone walls, maintaining the old farmhouse that had been deserted early in the century, digging a swimming hole and diverting water from Ball Mountain Brook to fill it. There was no tap water and no electricity, just a spring with a hand pump that once served the farm and kerosene lanterns. When we were not working, we were making near-lethal applejack from the crabapples that grew on the ancient trees in the meadow, shooting mice with slingshots, pretending to be pool sharks on a real felt-topped pool table whose origin was always a mystery to me, cooling off in the swimming hole, and, of course, reading comic books. I also spent many hours walking through the woods with this remarkable old man, learning not just the names of what lived on the mountain but how the pieces fit together.

After the camp was sold, some mammoth white pines were cut in the late 1950s for pulp, but the land then was resold to a respectful owner who was content to enjoy the forest and the meadow and to watch the old farm buildings rot into the landscape. The forest remains largely as it was, and so someday, perhaps, other city kids will come of age there.

I have returned to Sage Hill often since I was a child, just to refresh old memories. On one occasion, camped by the meadow's edge, I awoke at four in the morning to the undulating wailing of a pair of bobcats and noted with a groggy thrill that I was on the line of smell between these team hunters.

Even on these visits I still find myself in the grip of indeterminacy as I descend from the summit of this old hill. Within the clearing, however, where the old farm was until early in this century, fate has been ruling with an iron hand. Where once, as children, we ran through the tall timothy grass to a crabapple tree first base, now these hollowed and quixotic trees stand amid invading white pine saplings. At the margins of the old meadow, paper birch is now displacing the pines that, in turn, were encroaching on the meadow even forty years ago. And maples, beech, and oaks are beginning to take root among the birch and pines at the meadow's edge.

This is all as it should be according to the rules of plant succession in the ecology textbooks. In another couple of hundred years, in the unlikely event that the land remains undisturbed by people, tall hardwoods towering above a dank, tangled forest floor will have replaced the clearing that long ago was cut out of a similar forest.

Throughout New England, the forest has been invading abandoned meadows for the past one hundred years; gone are the days when the rocky soils of the northeastern United States were nearly all farmed or seeded for pasture and only scant forested land existed. In most of these vegetative battlegrounds, the invading trees now come from stands of second growth, and so those reclaimed forests may never look like the forests that once dominated the landscape. Sage Hill is somewhat unusual in that many of the invading platoons are remnants of old-growth forest, trees growing on land that was never clear-cut. With the exception of the meadows at the mountain's base, including the one in which the camp stood, Sage Hill generally escaped wholesale clear-cutting because sufficient flatter and more accessible lands for farming were available elsewhere.

Like a modern-day Noah's Ark, remnants of old-growth forest like that at Sage Hill contain the genetic material needed to someday restore the majestic forests of New England. But back in the days when New England was being clear-cut, did anyone foresee any reason other than convenience for leaving large stands of old-growth forest intact? Such stands must have seemed unkempt, an eyesore amid the neatly ordered fields. Who might have argued then that someday the floodwaters of New England agriculture would recede and those wild and unruly lands would enrich the lives of future generations?

The unknown hand that laid down the ax two hundred years ago, from whatever motive, deserves thanks. Mr. Smith also does, and for a similar reason, for he never tried to tame the wild and unruly in those bands of kids exploring the meadows and woods on Sage Hill. Just as the remnant old-growth forest on Sage Hill is now inexorably shaping the ecological succession of the land, so Mr. Smith's acceptance of the chaos within us shaped the trajectories of our lives. Perhaps that is why I still get a thrill out of having a mountain outsmart me and why I dread the thought of a world in which that opportunity no longer exists.

5

The Greatest Show on Earth

A peculiar dance was in progress. With a seemingly uncanny sense of timing, each performer approached and parted from first one and then another partner in endlessly varying, swaying, chiasmic rhythms. This was no ordinary production staged on a polished hardwood floor: the set was a foot-wide gap between a fallen, rotting tree trunk and the mulchy ground beneath. The dancers were scores of daddy longlegs, joined limb-to-limb to form a living web. By flexing and relaxing their legs, they created pulsating two-dimensional waves within a lacework that shimmered in the flashing specks of sunlight penetrating the verdant canopy high above.

In the tropical rain forests, pulsing conglomerations of life abound. If you sit in one spot and watch the canopy for glimpses of the brightly colored birds for which the tropics are famous, chances are you will sit for a while seeing nothing. But then, perhaps after ten mesmerizing minutes of staring at the fluttering foliage, you will suddenly first hear and then see a screaming frenzied flock of birds working their way overhead through the tall canopy. Then, in less than a minute, the flock moves on, and quiet sets in as fast as it was shattered.

Such flocking is an efficient way for birds to glean insects off the foliage and bark, because the bug that hops or flies away from one unlucky bird is likely to be snatched up by one nearby. Indeed, if the flock is large and contains a wide variety of bird species, the birds are probably going after insects as fruit-eating birds more rarely form large, mixed-species flocks.

While the frenzied screams of flocking birds and the moaning ululations of howling monkeys often comprise one's first impressions of animal life in the rain forest, patience and mental acclimatization reveal a profusion of more hidden life forms and behaviors, which, like the dancing daddy longlegs, are ultimately more memorable. There are the trapdoor spiders, living in steep earth embankments in holes closed off from the outside world by circular flaps of dried mud hinged to open outward. While the spiders know how to open them, their predators apparently do not. There is Albert's lyrebird, rarely seen but sometimes heard in a few patches of rain forest in eastern Australia. A superb auditory mimic, it can reproduce anything from the laughing peals of a kookaburra to the coughs of a passing hiker. There are giant fruit-eating bats, the flying foxes, found throughout the wet tropics of Asia and Australia. They resemble big, black, broken umbrellas caught in the treetops where they roost. There are the most hauntingly beautiful birds in the world, like the resplendent quetzal of Central America, the birds of paradise in tropical Asia, and the silktail of Fiji. You cannot help but shiver in awe when you first spot birds like these, probably after considerable searching through the thick forest growth. Other rain forest birds are not so much beautiful as bizarre, like the hornbills of Asia and Africa or the toucans of Central and South America.

The rain forest flora is no less fascinating. Shortly after enjoying the dancing web performance at La Selva, a tract of lowland rain forest set aside for biological research in Costa Rica, my wife and I sat on a riverbank, cooling our bare feet in the sluggish brown water. A kingfisher with a metallic green back and a chestnut band across the breast was doing a fine imitation of an air-to-sea missile as it repeatedly plummeted from a nearby branch. Suddenly, a sharp crack rang out, followed by a sequence of popping and swishing noises and then a thunderous crash. A giant fig tree had toppled, leaving a gaping sunny spot in the otherwise dense canopy.

A gap was formed, a noisy and dramatic but seemingly insignificant event in the life of a forest. In fact, tree fall in tropical forests is far from insignificant. Like presidential assassination, it is an event that alters the course of history, that shapes the future. In the gap created where the tree's tall canopy once shaded the forest floor, numerous tree seedlings, like opportunistic politicians, now have their moment in the sun. One of those seedlings is destined to outgrow the others and eventually fill in the hole in the canopy. Unlike most of the forests of the temperate and subarctic latitudes, which are dominated by a very few species of trees, the tropical rain forest is a mosaic of a huge variety of species. Any one tree is likely to be surrounded by a dozen or more different neighbors, so the seedling that ultimately wins the race to the canopy will not necessarily be the same type of tree that fell. The winner, too, perhaps a hundred years later, will fall, continuing the cycle of regrowth. This process of succession probably plays an important role in preventing a small number of tree species from becoming dominant. Gaps also help maintain the renowned diversity of animal species in the rain forest, both by maintaining tree diversity and more directly by providing temporarily open habitats in which there congregate an even greater variety of birds and other animals than is found in the dense forest.

In the wet and warm tropics, decay occurs rapidly, and so fallen trees and leaves from live trees do not last long on the forest floor. Thus, the soils in the tropics are often shallow, unlike the deep, rich soils that form in prairies, tundra, and boreal forests, where a colder climate slows the rate at which dead plant matter decays. In shallow soil, large trees cannot anchor to the ground with deep roots, so large live trees often fall rather than die and rot standing up. Many rain forest trees do, however, gain temporary respite from their horizontal fate because they are laced with giant vines, called lianas, to their neighbors or have formed finlike buttresses or multipod stilt roots above the ground. These buttresses and stilts also provide the growing tree with a means of taking up nutrients from a wider area of soil, a major advantage in the race to fill the gap first. Rapid decay, thin soils, gap formation, the race to fill gaps, roots designed to stabilize large trees and maximize nutrient uptake in thin soils—fused together, the coherence of these and other features of the rain forest are why our senses resonate with awe as we wander along the forest floor. These linked forms and fused processes are just as much a part of the biodiversity of the tropics as are the variety of species.

The term "biodiversity" requires a little explanation and apology. First, the apology. It is a terribly sterile, abstract word to describe something as fertile and tangible as the mosaic of life. Perhaps its icy aura makes it easier for people to talk about the loss of what it refers to, just as "body count" does in war.

There are three general kinds of biodiversity: habitat diversity, genetic diversity, and species diversity. The survival of each is linked to the health of the other two, and together they comprise the wealth of ecosystems discussed on our walk up Hidden Creek.

Habitat diversity refers to the variety of places where life exists—coral reefs, old-growth forests in the Pacific Northwest, tall grass prairie, coastal wetlands, and many others. Each broad type of habitat is the home for numerous species, most of which are utterly dependent on that habitat. So when a type of habitat disappears, a vast number of species disappear as well. More often, an entire habitat does not completely disappear but instead is nibbled away, acre by acre, until only small patches remain. This has happened to old-growth forest and coastal wetlands in the United States and is now in full swing in tropical forests throughout the world. Elimination of small patches of habitat can lead to the extinction of those species that live only in small regions of the habitat. Elimination of all but small patches is especially damaging because it not only eliminates many localized species but also threatens those species that are dependent on vast acreages for their survival.

To understand genetic diversity, it helps to first clarify what biologists mean when they refer to a "population." Consider the song sparrows in your neighborhood. They are a population—individuals of a species that live together, in the sense that mates are chosen from within the group. The sparrows in the population share more of their genes with each other than they do with other individuals from populations of the same species elsewhere, because individuals in one population rarely breed with those in another. Although each population within a species contains some genetic information unique to that population, individuals in all populations share in common the genetic information that defines their species.

In principle, individuals from one population could mate with individuals from another population of the same species. That is a definition of what a species is—a collection of individuals that could, in principle, interbreed. In practice, individuals from different populations within a species rarely interbreed because of geographic isolation.

The genetic diversity within a species is primarily the variety of populations that comprise it. Species reduced to a single population (like the California condor) generally contain less genetic diversity than those consisting of many populations. Song sparrows, found over much of North America, occur in numerous populations and thus maintain considerable genetic diversity within the species. Biologists care about the survival of populations, as well as species, because of the unique genetic information contained within populations.

The very survival of a species is dependent on the survival of its populations, for if only a few populations remain, there are few survival tactics that the species can deploy in the face of threats (such as global warming). Each population contains a distinct set of genetic instructions for how the species might adapt to threats. Nature, in other words, figured out long ago not to put all its eggs in one basket.

Finally, there is species diversity, which is what most people mean when they talk about biodiversity. The designation "species" is one level of classification in a taxonomic hierarchy that includes the genus, the family, the order, the class, the phylum, and the kingdom.[1]

There are about one and a half million named species on earth, but we know that many unnamed species exist, and the total number is probably between five and fifteen million. Most of the evidence for numerous unnamed species comes from studies of insects in tropical forests: when the canopy of a tropical tree is fumigated and all the dead insects collected, large numbers of hitherto unknown insects are frequently collected.

There are several hundred classes and several dozen phyla. Individuals in different classes differ from each other far more than do those in the same class but in different orders, families, or species. For example, a downy woodpecker and a mallard duck (both in the class Aves, which includes all the birds) are more alike than a tiger salamander and a wood rat (which are in the classes Amphibia and Mammalia, respectively). And individuals in different phyla differ from each other far more than those in the same phylum but in different classes. For example, salmon and horses (both in the phylum Chordata, or organisms

1. Consider people, whose species name is *Homo sapiens*. *Homo* is the genus, and *sapiens* designates the species. We happen, now, to be the only living species in the genus *Homo*. We are in the family Hominidae (apes and man), the order of Primates (lemurs, monkeys, apes, and man), the class Mammalia, the phylum Chordata (or vertebrates), and the kingdom animal.

with a spinal cord) are more alike than are spiders and worms (in the phyla Arthropoda and Annelida, respectively).

Tropical rain forests cover less than 2 percent of the planet and yet are the only home of at least 50 percent and possibly as many as 90 percent of all species on earth.[2] It has been estimated that in a typical acre of rain forest, there are likely to be more plant species than in all of Great Britain. Moreover, the geographic range of many species in the tropics is generally far smaller than it is in the temperate or polar latitudes. Thus, in the tropics, the species found in one acre differ from those in an adjacent acre far more than is the case elsewhere.

Why is the species diversity of tropical rain forests so high? Gap formation is not the only reason for the tremendous diversity of life in tropical forests, although it is the only one that virtually all ecologists agree is very important. Some ecologists argue that the benign environment of the tropics permits a diversity of life forms to coexist because it allows for highly specialized modes of existence. In the harsh climates encountered poleward of the tropics, organisms have to be "jacks-of-all-trades" so they can cope with hot and cold, wet and dry, long and short days. Intense specialization keeps organisms out of each other's way in the tropics, reducing competitive pressure. This argument has been criticized, however, on the grounds that the tropical environment is not as free of stress as the reasoning suggests: there are, critics claim, major seasonal fluctuations and randomly occurring disturbances (like gap formation) in the tropics, and these are, in effect, like the stresses encountered in temperate and even subarctic lands.

An argument that diversity can pull itself up by its bootstraps, that diversity begets diversity, might also have some merit. More plant species on an acre of land means that more insect and bird species can each find their special food source and thus that they do not need to compete with one another. Less obvious, more species of predators means a greater diversity of prey. A species of prey might not gather food as well as the next, but if it can avoid its particular predator better, then it can still have an edge over its competitors.

2. The higher estimate is based on the assumption that a large share of the to-be-discovered species will be tropical because biological exploration of the tropics is so fragmentary. Other habitats are also poorly explored, though, and undoubtedly contain numerous species unknown to science today. Among these are the soils of temperate forests, such as the moist old-growth forests in the Pacific Northwest of the United States, where numerous new species of fungi, nematodes, beetles, and other equally warm and cuddly soil dwellers are likely to lurk.

The question of why there are so many species in the tropics has two facets. One is the issue we have been addressing: how can all those species maintain themselves against the extinguishing forces of competition, predation, and environmental stress? The other is, how did all the species now inhabiting tropical forests either first evolve there or arrive on the scene from elsewhere? Our attempt to answer the first question with "diversity begets diversity" is fine; but it is uselessly circular when applied to the second question, for which we turn to the ice ages to find one possible answer.

During geologic periods such as the present, when the great ice sheets that cover the high latitudes during ice ages are in retreat, many species that live far outside the tropics are, in a sense, living on borrowed time. The ice will return some day, and when it does, many species of the temperate and polar latitudes will either perish from cold or move equatorward. So the tropics receive a regular influx of species, whereas the higher latitudes periodically suffer a loss of species. For at least the past several million years, major ice ages have occurred roughly every hundred thousand years, with minor ice ages occurring more frequently. Thus, there have been recurring episodes that deplete the species abundance of the temperate and polar zones relative to that of the tropics.

This argument seems to be capable of proving the opposite as well: the tropics should be species-poor because during the warm interglacial periods, many species living in the tropics will either perish from excessive heat or move poleward. Which, if either, version of the argument is valid? One important fact bearing on this question is the brevity of interglacial periods compared to ice ages. We, living today at a warm time, tend to think that ice ages are an occasional interruption; in fact, for at least the last few million years, they were the norm, with brief interruptions of warm interglacial conditions. Moreover, the temperature difference between ice ages and interglacial periods is far greater in the temperate and polar regions than in the tropics. So the pressure exerted on temperate species to migrate toward the tropics during ice ages probably greatly exceeds that on tropical species to migrate poleward during interglacial periods. Thus, the original argument is more likely to be valid than the flip-side argument.

Ecologists have also argued that the tropics should be especially species-rich because the evolution of new species (called speciation) ought to be occurring most rapidly there. In the temperate, subarctic, and arctic zones, summer-winter climate swings often cause animals (at least nonhibernators) to migrate large distances to seek favorable seasonal climate conditions year-round. Moreover, large animals tend to have larger home ranges outside the tropics (where food is generally less abundant, forcing animals to wander farther for a meal). Conversely, this translates into less intermingling and more isolation of populations within species indigenous to the tropics. Isolated populations speciate more rapidly than those that intermingle, in somewhat the same way that a small group of children who always play together in isolation tend to develop unique code words and play habits.

Each year, during the past several decades, people have been destroying enough tropical forest to cover an area the size of the state of Pennsylvania. Some of this lost forest, particularly in Central and South America, is burned and then used for cattle grazing or for crops; some, particularly in Asia, is clear-cut for its timber; and, particularly in Africa, fuelwood gathering accelerates the pace of deforestation. Since the turn of the century, between one-fourth and one-half of the rain forests on earth have been destroyed. At the current rate of destruction, there will be only tiny protected patches of rain forest left by the middle of the twenty-first century.

Because of the tremendous concentration of species in the tropics and their often narrow geographic ranges, biologists estimate that tropical deforestation will result in the loss of half or more of the existing species on earth during the next seventy-five years. To put this in perspective, it is useful to look at prehistoric rates of extinction. Prior to the burgeoning of humanity on earth, species probably disappeared at the average rate of about one per year. Sometimes the rate was much higher; at other times it was lower. Sixty-five million years ago, an "extinction event" occurred, in which not only the dinosaurs disappeared but as many as a quarter of all the species on earth as well. The fossil record suggests that on a geologic time scale, the disappearances took place rapidly, perhaps in less than a few thousand years. That event was probably caused by an extraterrestrial object (an asteroid, for example) slamming into our planet and thereby creating environmental havoc.

There are numerous ways in which the impact could have stressed the planetary environment so as to bring about the extinction of many species. As the object passed down through the atmosphere, the frictional heat it produced would have converted some of the nitrogen in the atmosphere into nitric acid, thereby causing an intense acid rain episode over much of the planet. The debris strewn up into the atmosphere on impact would have blocked sunlight for several years and severely cooled the planet. If, as believed, the impact occurred on a site with carbonate bedrock, massive amounts of carbon dioxide would have been released into the atmosphere, causing an intense greenhouse warming. While we do not know whether the warming or the cooling from these last two mechanisms predominated, it is highly unlikely that they miraculously canceled each other out.

Whatever the direct stresses that led to the extinction of the dinosaurs and other organisms, that extinction event was only one of many that have occurred over geologic time. The fossil record suggests that such major gaps in life on earth happen roughly every one hundred million years, with less dramatic extinction events occurring perhaps every twenty to forty million years. Between these extinction events, new species evolve to fill the gaps.

The aftermath of an extinction event may be an opportune time for speciation. Once the dust settles, the carbon dioxide is absorbed into the oceans, and the rain is no longer too acidic, there are numerous recently vacated niches for new species to fill. Yet we argued earlier that diversity begets diversity, that niches are often not passive "filing folders" into which species are placed but rather derive from living species. If this is so, then it is not clear that the aftermath of an extinction event is necessarily a time of rapid speciation. It is true that mammals might have evolved when they did (at the end of the age of dinosaurs) because the dinosaurs were no longer around to eat them, but had the food sources of the emerging mammals been decimated, it is doubtful the mammals would have been successful then. In any event, whether speciation occurs in bursts or in a slow, steady fashion, it is inherently a slower process than extinction caused by asteroid impacts or the rapid deforestation taking place today. Moreover, few biologists would argue that a sugarcane field sprayed with herbicides and pesticides is as congenial a site for successful speciation (of anything other than chemically tolerant weeds and pests) as was the forest that the field replaced.

So we see that humanity is now in the process of destroying roughly as many species during the next fifty to one hundred years as were wiped out every one hundred million years by natural causes. It takes only a few decades, as history shows, to drive a once-abundant species, like the passenger pigeon, to extinction. It is inconceivable that during the coming millennia, evolution could replace with new species those lost to deforestation and other human actions.

Rain forest destruction not only will wipe out species in the tropics but will have global repercussions as well. One of the first hints of such a repercussion first unfolded in the late 1970s, when bird-watchers in the United States and Europe began to observe a decline in the numbers of certain birds in spring and summer. For many of us, the first accounts of these declines seemed like a gruesome reminder of an earlier story, one that truly ushered in, over thirty years ago, the modern era of environmental science and action. Let us take a quick look at that bit of history before coming back to its recent echo.

In 1962, Rachel Carson warned the world, with her landmark book *Silent Spring,* that the time was approaching when spring would no longer be a season filled with bird song. Pesticides, she said, were killing birds, and unless we found substitutes for chemical pesticides, they might kill us as well. Soon thereafter, the scientific evidence became indisputable that one particular pesticide, DDT, was responsible for driving certain species to the brink of extinction. The greatest damage was not to songbirds, however, but to bald eagles, ospreys, brown and white pelicans, peregrine falcons, and other species we rarely hear in our backyards.

One of the pieces of evidence that clinched the DDT story was data showing declines in the numbers of certain vulnerable species of birds. This evidence came in large part from the remarkable efforts of thousands of amateur bird-watchers around the world. The other two were measurements of abnormally high levels of DDT in the tissue of birds undergoing a decline in numbers and identification of a mechanism by which DDT could cause mortality. All three pieces of evidence were in hand by the late 1960s. The primary mechanism turned out to be eggshell thinning, induced by high DDT levels that caused eggs to break before embryos were ready to hatch. Abnormally high levels of DDT were found, as expected, in the tissue of birds that feed at the tops of long food chains.

DDT is now banned, at least in the United States, but the observations of bird-watchers are once again indicating declines in the numbers of various species of birds. This time it is not the eagles, hawks, and pelicans that are on the decline; their populations are actually recovering because of the pesticide ban. The victims today are warblers, tanagers, flycatchers, orioles, vireos, thrushes—the songbirds Carson warned about. What is going on?

These declining songbirds share a trait: they are migrants, spending spring and summer in the woods, fields, and gardens of North America but migrating south each fall to the tropics of Central and South America. The evidence is not all in yet, but deforestation in the tropics is probably an important cause of the songbird population declines. There can be little doubt that loss of nesting habitats in the United States is also contributing to the declines.

Excellent records of bird populations are also available from the many bird-watchers in Europe. Bird populations have declined there as well, although the problem does not appear to be as severe as in the United States. This may be because European migrants use African forests for wintering grounds to a lesser extent than U.S. migrants use the tropical forests of Central and South America. And at least some of the European declines appear to be linked to drought in northern Africa rather than to deforestation in the central African tropics.

The juxtaposition of the DDT story and the more recent deforestation story drives home an important message: the world is a small place, and it is getting smaller. DDT traveled by wind, rain, and river from the farms in the interior of the United States to distant lakes and to the estuaries of our coastline where it contaminated fish and ultimately birds that prey on fish. The idea that a pollutant could be wafted across the nation was at first greeted with skepticism, because the prevailing view prior to the 1970s was that pollutants used locally only cause damage locally. Some DDT did show up in the arctic and antarctic, but serious damage was confined to continental distances. By the early 1970s, even pesticide manufacturers were convinced that a thousand miles of desert or a mountain range is not a barrier to the transport of DDT. The recent songbird decline carries an even more ominous message. The entire globe is one interconnected system; the crash of a felled tree in the tropics is heard around the world.

But why should tropical deforestation concern us so much? After all, some pesticides can harm our health, whereas the decline of our songbirds in spring is merely a loss of some pleasure in our lives. The temptation to reply with a simple "Merely?" is strong, but, in fact, the repercussions of tropical deforestation go far beyond loss of numerous individual species, tropical or otherwise, as a bird's-eye view of the Amazon recently reminded me.

While flying over hundreds of miles of the Amazon Basin in 1989, I was shocked by what I saw below. While most of the ground was obscured from my vision because of heavy cloud cover, here and there it could be seen through holes where the clouds were parted. And on those patches of visible ground, the forest was mostly gone, replaced by clear-cuts, plantations, roads, and settlements. My first reaction was to deduce that nearly all the forest must be gone, for if my poll of the ground cover was reliable, that conclusion clearly followed. Was the widely reported estimate that about 10 percent of the Amazonian forest has been cut in recent decades a gross underestimate?

I quickly realized that polling ground cover by looking through holes in the clouds is somewhat like polling people at a golf course about their political preferences; it is a poll based on a biased sample. While relieved that deforestation had not progressed to the level I had initially deduced, I was still not at all pleased by the situation. The very cause of the bias, I realized, is itself cause for alarm. My sample was biased because holes in the clouds are more likely to appear above patches of deforested land than above untouched forest. Why? Because the clouds are created by the forest. Remove the forests, and you eliminate the clouds above them.

Why is this a cause for alarm? Trees, like joggers on a hot day, keep cool by sweating. In the case of vegetation, sweating is called transpiration. Each year, the trees on earth transpire to the atmosphere about ten thousand cubic miles of water,[3] all of which falls back to earth as rain or snow. A large share of that transpiration comes from tropical rain forests. An acre of such forest transpires nearly ten thousand gallons of water each day, which is about three times the evaporation rate from an average acre of ocean surface. And when the vast amounts of

3. This is a volume of water one and a half times greater than that in the Great Lakes of the United States and Canada or, equivalently, an amount roughly equal to the annual discharge to the sea of all the world's rivers.

transpired water from the tropics rise high enough into the atmosphere, they condense and form the dense cloud covers so often observed there.

From the air above, clouds look quiescent, but in fact they are nearly always in a state of flux, formed by condensation and wrung out as rain. Water transpired from the Amazonian interior is likely to fall as rain downwind but still well within the basin. A water molecule is likely to be recycled in this way several times before eventually raining or flowing out to sea. Thus, the rain that sustains life in the forests of one part of the Amazonian forest is likely to owe its existence to the transpiring forest upwind. The influence of rain forest transpiration extends even farther, however, for the monsoon rains that permit agriculture throughout much of central Asia, including India, originate, in part, from transpiration in the tropical rain forests of Africa.

Staring down on the cloud cover above the Amazon Basin, my eyes began to hurt from the glare of sunlight reflected off the top of the clouds. The reflected sunlight is largely headed off to space and thus does not warm the earth. Were the clouds absent, the light would be mostly absorbed by the ground, where it would increase the temperature of the already hot tropics. Thus, deforestation causes heating by eliminating the cloud cover that shades the ground.[4]

To this source of heating in the aftermath of deforestation must be added a second and a third. The second is a direct effect of eliminating the transpiring trees. It is not just the trees that keep cool by transpiration; the process cools the surrounding air as well, and so reduced transpiration means higher temperature.

The third reason that deforestation heats the climate is more global in scope. When trees are cut and all or some of the wood and foliage is left to rot, the carbon in the tree is oxidized to carbon dioxide. Since about one-third of a tree, by weight, is carbon, a good deal of carbon dioxide can be produced when a large area of forest is felled. Even if the cleared land is planted with crops, the carbon that can be stored in cropland is vastly less than that in the forest it replaced. In recent years, worldwide deforestation is resulting in the conversion of one or two billion tons of tree carbon to carbon dioxide, thereby adding significantly to the roughly six billion tons of carbon released to the atmo-

4. A different view of the effect of deforestation on climate is sometimes advanced. Deforestation, the argument goes, will result in a cooling because the relatively bare ground that results from clear-cutting provides a more reflecting surface than does thick dark forest. While it is true that bare ground often reflects more sunlight than forest does, the change in cloud cover is likely to alter the fate of sunlight over the forest far more than is the change in the darkness of the ground cover.

sphere as carbon dioxide by fossil fuel burning. By contributing to the buildup of carbon dioxide in the atmosphere, deforestation is one of the contributors to the impending global warming.

The tropical forests have been referred to as "the lungs of the world," a phrase sometimes interpreted to mean that if these forests are cut down, then people will not have enough oxygen to breathe. This is somewhat of a misconception. Picture a forest that has been around for a long time. Trees die, and new ones take their place. During the growing life of a tree, it is indeed pumping oxygen into the atmosphere in exchange for carbon dioxide, which it removes from the atmosphere to meet its carbon needs. But at the same time, somewhere else in the forest, dead trees are rotting and in the process adding carbon dioxide back to the atmosphere, while removing atmospheric oxygen. The oxygen budget works out neatly: the amount of oxygen a tree adds to the atmosphere during its life just equals the amount it removes when it rots. So unless the forest is growing in bulk (that is, there is more growth than death and rotting), a forest produces no net amount of oxygen. By the same token, if the forest is clear-cut and the dead trees either are burned or rot, then oxygen is removed from the atmosphere. Fortunately, even if all the vegetation on earth were cut and burned and no new plant growth were permitted, we would only lose about a tenth of a percent of our atmosphere's oxygen supply (although we would, of course, all starve to death).

Just as deforestation alters climate, so global warming is virtually certain to further accelerate the rate of extinction of tropical species brought about initially by deforestation. Consider the dipterocarps, a family of trees that includes the mahoganies and that contains about 80 percent of all the large trees growing in the tropics of Asia. Asian dipterocarps do not flower and set seed every year; triggered by occasional cold snaps that are not likely to occur annually, reproduction occurs only once or twice a decade.[5] These occasional cold snaps will likely occur less frequently under conditions of global warming, thereby

5. There is a good reason that individual plants might not produce seeds every year but only at longer intervals and then in synchrony with the others in the neighborhood. It is unlikely that seed eaters could store enough seeds to last several years, and so no predator can rely solely on a species of tree that reproduces only occasionally. Moreover, when the trees do set seed in synchrony, so many seeds are produced that the predators are overwhelmed by the abundance and cannot possibly eat them all. Thus, reproduction is assured. Bamboo epitomizes this strategy, for some bamboo reproduce in synchrony at intervals of many decades. The sensitivity of Asian dipterocarps to global warming was explained to me by Stephen Hubbell, a Princeton University ecologist who specializes in tropical forest ecology.

placing in jeopardy the future reproductive success of a large family of trees that are not only a cornerstone of tropical Asian ecosystems but a major economic resource of that region as well.

In addition to caring about the survival of tropical forests for purely aesthetic reasons and because of their influence on regional and global climate, there are a host of other selfish reasons for people to be concerned about their destruction. Few people are aware that wheat, corn, rice, and all our other food crops originated from localized populations of wild species. And about 80 percent of all these crops came originally from the tropics. Corn came from South American forests, potatoes from the Andes, sugar from India, rice from Asian forests, and even the chicken from the Asian tropics.[6]

Future crops, as well, will come from such sources. For example, in the mountains of Mexico, a variety of corn that can fix atmospheric nitrogen and thus does not require chemical fertilizer was recently discovered. The variety has the added benefit of being a perennial, in contrast to our present commercial varieties of corn, which are annuals and therefore must be reseeded each year. The unique set of genes that governs this property of the wild corn population has proven difficult to genetically engineer, but now this wild corn variety might be domesticated and the crop used to feed future generations. Ironically, the wild land where this population grows was slated to be cleared for conventional agriculture when the corn variant was discovered.

It would be foolish to assume that humanity's need for new kinds of food crops has ended and that we need never turn again to the tropics for new varieties of edible plants. New pests evolve, in defense against which we constantly need new crop strains. Moreover, the impending greenhouse climate, unprecedented as it is in human history, will increase our need for genetic varieties of plants that can tolerate hot conditions. We had better preserve the rain forests, since we are not going to find these varieties in the arctic. Nor will genetic engineers "invent" needed new genetic combinations from scratch; even the advances in crop strains produced by these engineers will continue to derive from the genetic possibilities found in nature.

Medicine, as well as agriculture, has benefited enormously from natural ecosystems, especially from rain forests. As visitors to tropical rain forests can easily imagine, plants growing on the rain forest floor face

6. A more complete and very readable discussion of the agricultural and medical benefits that humanity has derived from tropical rain forests can be found in *Tropical Rainforests,* by Arnold Newman (New York and Oxford: Facts on File, 1990).

a perpetual threat from insect attack. Under such circumstances, it is small wonder that many plants have evolved defensive strategies to protect them from being nibbled away. Often, these defenses consist of noxious chemicals. Fortunately for us, what is noxious to a bug has a good chance of also being noxious to a bacterium, a virus, or a cancer cell.

Hodgkin's disease was once nearly always fatal. But then in the 1950s, the rosy periwinkle, a seemingly insignificant flower growing in the forests of Madagascar, was found to contain certain chemicals, called alkaloids, that proved effective in treating the disease. Now, of course, scientists can culture the cells of this plant and extract the curative alkaloids; but we never would have had the opportunity to do this if the species had been destroyed before we discovered its benefits. Other cancers as well, such as lymphocytic leukemia, are treated with drugs derived from the periwinkle. Where once children could look forward to only a 20-percent chance of recovering from this leukemia, today the odds are about 99 percent.

Today, about half the drugs used in the Western world are derived from plants, and over half of those come from the tropics. Quinine for treating malaria and other ills comes from the cinchona tree of the Andean tropical forests. Diosgenin, a source of cortisone used to treat Addison's disease, rheumatoid arthritis, sciatica, colitis, and many other diseases, comes from the Mexican yam. Worldwide, about $50 billion a year are spent on drugs derived from rain forests. Although the medicinal value of over 99 percent of all tropical plants has not yet even been explored, the screening that has taken place reveals that about 5 percent show some promise in this regard. Future drugs for treating AIDS, Alzheimer's disease, numerous currently untreatable cancers, and other scourges may well be lurking in the rain forests today. With every acre of lost rain forest, there is lost opportunity to save human lives.

It is not only the forests of the developing nations that contain the promise of new drugs. In the Pacific Northwest of the United States, the old-growth forest (a nontropical rain forest) is the scene of an interesting interplay of economic and social forces. Lumber companies want to cut timber there, while advocates for endangered species have fought this in an effort to save the rare spotted owl that breeds only in that habitat. But now a new participant has entered the fray. Drug companies are eyeing, with huge profits in mind, the Pacific yew, a "weed" species of tree that only grows there. In its bark is a chemical, taxol, that appears to be a surprisingly effective treatment for several cancers, such as ovarian, breast, and lung, that are now among the most deadly. Perhaps someday we will look back in gratitude to the spotted owl for providing the initial rallying point for a conservation effort that ultimately preserved not just a unique habitat but also a medical bonanza for humanity—one that far exceeds in value the benefits of a one-shot timber harvest of old growth.

Both the medical and the agricultural uses of wild species underscore the necessity of protecting populations, not just species. It is likely that drug company scientists studying the bark of the yew tree will discover variations in its effectiveness from one population of the trees to another. For that reason, alone, it is not adequate to simply ensure that some trees survive for plantation-style commercialization of the species. Such plantations would likely be genetic monocultures, and there is no way to know in advance that the best genes will have been selected for the purpose. Even if it someday becomes possible to copy nature and artificially produce taxol, perhaps in forms that are more effective at treating cancer than those derived directly from the yew trees, it still would be foolish to clear-cut the forests, for we know so little of the additional treasures for humanity waiting there to be discovered.

Wildlife conservation movements throughout the world have focused their efforts primarily on animals like pandas, cranes, ocelots, and spotted owls—animals that generate the interest and sympathy of virtually everyone. Thanks to the breadth of endangered species protection legislation in the United States, occasionally a conservation battle is joined over more obscure species such as a little fish or a scruffy plant. But when it comes to obscurity, it is hard to beat the nematodes, fungi, beetles, bacteria, mites, and other soil dwellers of forest and grassland soils. Along with many forms of nonedible and nonplayful marine life, these organisms have been largely neglected by scientists and conservation organizations alike,[7] despite the fact that their roles in the ecosystems they inhabit and the direct benefits they could someday confer on humanity have hardly been explored.

For many people, the selfish reasons—aesthetic pleasure, new cures for illness, new food crops, maintenance of ecosystem services, and income

7. An exception is the Xerces Society, which although emphasizing butterfly conservation, is also devoting resources to other invertebrate conservation projects.

from tourism—for saving species are sufficient in themselves. Arguments for protecting species based on such reasons appeal particularly to many economists and others who seek to base decision-making on cost-benefit comparisons that operate within a free market. Unfortunately, there is scant evidence to date that the full economic benefits of healthy ecosystems can be either calculated or somehow reflected automatically in the prices of things. This is not for want of effort, however, for numerous attempts have been made to come up with monetary estimates of the value of pleasure and even of human life. But none of these estimates seems as acceptable as, for example, the price of cheese in the marketplace.

A growing number of people, however, approach the issue from a different perspective, arguing that the question is not one of costs and benefits but rather one of right and wrong. It is fundamentally immoral and unjust, in this view, for people to cause extinction of species—at any price.

The first view is relativistic (monetary costs are always relative) and unabashedly anthropocentric; the second is absolutist and nature-centric. Between them lies an amalgamation that is based on the moral ground of the second viewpoint but that is anthropocentric like the first. To wit: individuals and nations have no right to commit the immoral act of depriving humanity, including future generations, of the ecological wealth (in all senses of the term) with which we have been endowed through the ages. The translation of this abstraction into action might still occur in the marketplace, where consumer choices are driven by conscience as well as prices (the simplistic vision of much economic theory to the contrary), but it would also occur in the political arena, fueled by the power of education, religion, and enlightened self-interest.

To slow the rate of tropical deforestation and thereby preserve species and slow global warming, incentive schemes are needed to entice developing countries to preserve their rich biological heritage of tropical forests. Sure, those incentives will cost the rich nations money, but so will global warming and loss of valuable genetic material. Commercial hardwoods can be grown on plantations dedicated to that purpose rather than ripped out of virgin forest, but we may have to pay a little more for that mahogany tabletop that comes from a plantation. What is the alternative? Most likely, it will be cheaper mahogany for a few more decades as we destroy the remaining tropical forests, a miserably hot climate in the near future, and, eventually, no more mahogany anyway when the forests are all gone. Similarly, we will have to help subsidize the improvement of agricultural productivity on lands that have already been cleared and promote the reforestation of deforested sites throughout the world where erosion and infertility have destroyed their use for agriculture.

Perhaps we have to go further, however, and help provide conservation incentives to both governments and forest dwellers in the tropics. Drug companies that now derive tremendous profits from the living products of tropical forests often do not properly reward the tribes or nations that own these resources. Perhaps developing nations with rich genetic resources in their forests can regain control of their biological heritages. If profits from nondestructive uses of forests increased, then there would be less incentive to seek profit from destructive uses. Cartel formation is one approach, although an "OGEC," or Organization of Gene-Exporting Countries, is not likely to be any more successful than are the OPEC nations with petroleum pricing.

A recent collaboration between the Merck drug company and Costa Rica's Institute for Biodiversity (INBio) is an innovative and promising attempt to deal with these issues. INBio, a private research organization, will provide Merck with samples of tropical plants and insects and share in the eventual profits. In the long run, Costa Rica hopes to develop its own capability to extract and market drugs from the forests, and some Costa Rican nationals hope that the arrangement with Merck will expedite that goal. Critics argue, however, that the uniqueness of individual patches of forest habitat and the small ranges of many tropical species suggest that a more localized approach—one that keeps control in the hands of forest dwellers rather than nations' capitals—might be more successful.

A recent study[8] of the economic value of a patch of Amazonian rain forest compared the profit that could accrue from clear-cutting the forest with that from harvesting forest products that the trees produce year after year (or the "sustainable yield," to use the current buzzword). Averaged over many years, the sustainable harvesting of the forest was shown to yield greater profit. One problem, though, is that the study was only carried out for one little area of the Amazonian forest. Were many people in many areas to attempt to make a living by the same strategy, the markets for some of these sustainable products might satu-

8. C. P. Peters, A. H. Gentry, and R. O. Mendelsohn, "Valuation of an Amazonian Rainforest," *Nature* 339 (1989):655–656.

rate, and the profits would drop sharply. Another problem is that starving people are likely to opt for land use that provides the quickest source of income, regardless of its long-term implications. Nevertheless, this study points the way toward what must surely be part of any long-term solution to saving biodiversity—the development of sustainable methods of profiting from our natural resources.

In 1984, Thomas Lovejoy, then vice president for science of the World Wildlife Fund and now foreign secretary of the Smithsonian Institution, came up with a superb idea for protecting tropical forests. Many nations that are in possession of bountiful tropical forest resources are also deeply in debt to the rich nations. Banks holding these debts generally have little hope that the debts will be recovered. Lovejoy suggested that the rich nations swap debt for nature. In other words, they cancel debt in return for a commitment by the developing nations to protect their own forests. To make this attractive to the holders of the debt, they would be reimbursed for at least some portion of the amount owed them, which is better than getting nothing back. The reimbursement would come from either private groups or from governments of the rich nations that recognize the global benefits of saving biodiversity.

Debt reduction will also bring its own benefits to the rain forests. Nations deeply in debt are likely to place more emphasis on cash crops for sale overseas than on sustainable yields of foods and materials for the use of local village populations. The clearing of large areas of land for such cash crops is often the motive for deforestation.

Although deforestation in the species-rich tropics is currently a focus for outrage, it must never be forgotten that deforestation in North America and Europe has destroyed even larger areas of old-growth forest than in the tropics. Virtually all the magnificent hardwood forests of the northeastern United States were cleared prior to the Civil War; the second-growth forests that have sprouted on abandoned farmland during the past century are a poor ecological substitute for what was lost. In recent years, clear-cutting in the United States is again destroying some of the most magnificent old-growth forest in the world. In the late 1980s, it looked as though we were going to destroy for timber all of the magnificent Alaskan Tongass rain forest. Fortunately, in 1990, the U.S. government (led by Senator Timothy Wirth of Colorado and Representative George Miller of California) enacted legislation that protected what remained of that spectacular national forest, the largest in the United States. Thanks to Wirth and Miller, we now need not feel quite so embarrassed asking tropical nations to protect their forests; nevertheless, as of this writing, timber interests still threaten the scattered remnants of old-growth forest in Oregon, Washington, and California. Surely the most important action that the rich nations can take is to set their own houses in order. Only the most naive could believe that we can happily proceed to clear-cut our forests of the Pacific Northwest and at the same time successfully exhort our global neighbors to the south to save theirs.

Each year, millions of trees go up in smoke in the Brazilian Amazon so that more land can be converted to plantation or ranchland; nowhere on the planet is the metaphor of burning dynamite fuses more manifest. Nowhere are forces blasting the roots of trees so much as in Asia, where vast amounts of forest get sliced up into furniture, siding, chopsticks, and pulp. Throughout central Africa, where forests are stripped practically bare for fuelwood by an energy-hungry people, the boundary between life and death is paper thin—not as in Dylan Thomas's lovely images but as in sheer horror, pain, and gut-wrenching hunger for millions of children. And in the rich nations, which should be the origin of forces for global fusion, for a uniting of energies and a sharing of wealth in pursuit of the global good, our current actions, sadly, speak louder than our words.

6

Between the Devil and the Deep Blue Sea

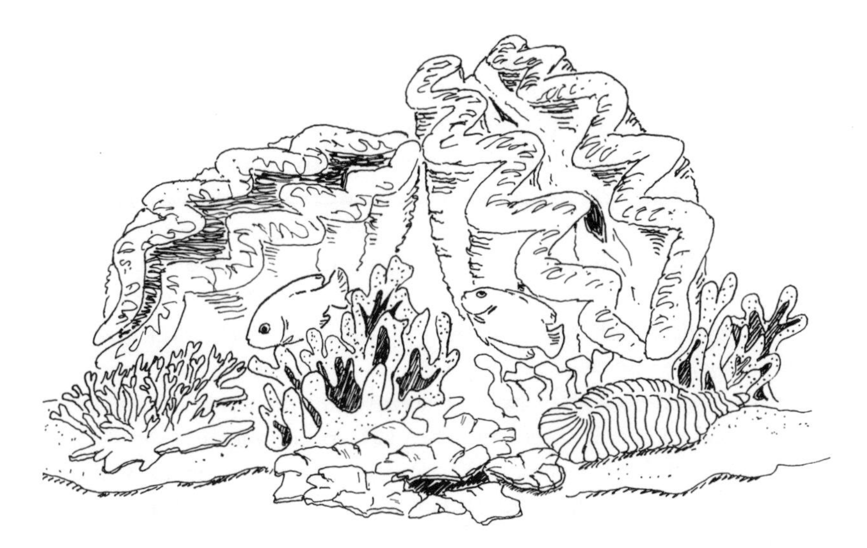

When the tidal curtain lifts at Pulau Dua, an island in the Java Sea, a bizarre matinee can often be witnessed. The protagonists enter stage from the seaward door in narrow channels on the exposed mud flats that fill with the receding waters. Their costume and makeup artist is truly inspired, for these creatures have red polka dots splashed across their streamlined blue-gray bodies, spiny sails on their backs that can be raised or lowered on demand, bulging eye buds, and gaping frog mouths.

As the stage fills, the action begins. Pairing off with their nearest neighbors, the larger ones raise their fins, rear out of the water, arch their heads, feint right and left, and lunge forward to batter each other's heads. Occasionally, in respite from the battles, they lower their fins and squirm around on the soft mud, where they munch on the abundant crabs and other crustacea lurking there. During these intermissions, periscopic eye buds often protrude above the water, ever watchful for aggressors. In contrast to the nearly two-foot-long fighting grown-ups, the smaller ones, only a few inches long, simply feed the whole time. Whether the splashing and commotion from the battles scares up food from the mud or warns the crustacea to burrow deeper is unclear.

During the hour of lowest tide, the fighting and feeding continue. A few of these mud skippers, as the creatures are called, emerge as victors, beating back all who contest their little patch of otherwise undistinguished feeding territory. Then, as the curtain begins to fall, they all swim off into the swelling waters.

Pulau Dua means Bird Island in Indonesian, and indeed the treetops are as full of bird life as the mud flats are of aquatic life. The island is a rookery for herons, bitterns, and egrets. During the nesting season, the trees are festooned with dozens of elegantly plumaged adult birds. When the hatchlings emerge, there is a constant daytime din of gibbering young demanding food from their harried elders. The latter cruise back and forth from nests to sea, bringing gulletfuls of fish every half hour or so.

A forty-foot-high platform on a bird observation tower was the roost on which my wife and I elected to spend the nights during our visit there in 1986 with "Chuck" Darsano, an Indonesian naturalist active in local conservation efforts. The platform commands a spectacular view of Pulau Dua's treetops. At sunset, as we sat in our roost, thousands of these huge, graceful birds returned to theirs, the last rounds of the day completed.

The sunset was splendid, but it surely paled in comparison to the sunsets seen at Pulau Dua one hundred years earlier. The island is located off the northern shore of the western tip of Java, within easy earshot of any eruptions in the chain of offshore volcanoes that include Krakatoa. For several years after Krakatoa's giant 1883 eruption, the debris it produced lingered in the air around the world, prismatically displaying the colors of the setting sun.

Besides two observation towers, the only other work of humanity on the island was a stone lean-to for campers. Its stones were carved out of dead coral reef dug from the island's "bedrock." Once a living, submerged reef, Pulau Dua probably met the fate of many reefs that once existed—death by siltation. Corals drown in silt the way we drown in water, or fish in air. Where once a live reef supported a dazzling array of fish, coral, and crustacea, now its corpse catches the mud in which the skippers feed and binds the soil on which grow the trees where the wading birds breed.

In death, then, coral reefs provide for life. But even more intricate and exquisite is the way a living reef provides for its own survival and growth. Such reefs exemplify the balance of nature. Often misunderstood to mean that nature is unchanging (it never is), the balance of nature has at its core harmonious and productive integration, the working together of the pieces to achieve a synthesis that is fitter and more capable of carrying out more functions than the pieces individually.

Corals are tiny animals. They live colonially in geometrically arrayed spaces embedded in limestone formed from their bodily secretions. These housing projects come in a dazzling variety of shapes and colors and are often fused together into gigantic reefs stretching tens of miles along coastlines and from the surface of the sea down to a hundred feet or more in clear water. When sea level is rising slowly enough, over the millennia, new reef can be built on top of old, so that the dead reef can be several thousand feet thick.

The complexity of a healthy coral reef is a feast for the eyes. To snorkel or dive in its waters is to enter a fantastical world in slow motion. Typically, at any productive reef, hundreds of different species of fish of brilliant colors and bizarre shapes glide by in slow procession, pausing occasionally to nibble at the coralline carpet or to devour smaller fish. Giant clams over a meter wide, electric blue starfish and lavender sea cucumbers, yellow fan-shaped and purple cup-shaped sponges, intricately patterned cone shells, huge rays with bright blue polka dots, shrimps with brilliant red stripes—all share this Seussian universe.

In many species of coral, the individual animals farm the space within their own bodies. In a marvelous example of integration, microscopic algae dwell within the coral. Like other algae, this species is capable of converting sunlight, carbon dioxide, and nutrients in the water, such as nitrogen and phosphorus, into more algae. The coral's digestive products are a rich source of the nitrogen, in the form of ammonia, needed for algal growth. Because ammonia levels are far higher within the coral than they are in the seawater outside, the algae greatly benefit by foregoing the freedom of the open sea. And what do the corals get out of this arrangement? First, the digestive juices of the coral cause glycerol, an energy-rich carbohydrate, to leak from the algae. Thus, for the coral, algal growth is food on the table. Second, like any animal, corals can be poisoned by the ammonia they excrete as a waste product; the algae serve as little waste treatment plants, converting the poison into food. Like the lichens, the integration of the coral and the algae is a splendid symbiosis.

Other reef animals also cultivate algae. The giant clams do it—growing the same algal species that the coral farm—on their fleshy outer lips. The true pioneers of this approach to life are some evolutionarily ancient sponges, the first multicelled animals, who cultivate the even more ancient blue-green algae within their convoluted interiors.

The types of symbiosis found in reefs are not limited to algal farming. A few species of sponges exert an extraordinary influence on the architecture of their larger reef community. Coral colonies grow by secreting limestone protrusions into available spaces, thereby creating complex shapes and fragile structures, an underseascape of steep convoluted pinnacles and canyons. As the sponges bore into the new coral heads to create protected living space, the loose limestone "tailings" they produce fill up the canyons around the protrusions. Parrot fish and other coral predators also produce sandy limestone debris as they scrape away at the live coral heads in search of juicy coral polyps. This loose material is then bonded with limestone secretions produced by free-living algae (not those living within the bodies of the coral) to create the large sturdy assemblages we call reefs. It is doubtful that reefs would have the strength to withstand the buffeting of waves if this gradual filling in, this flattening, of the new reef surface did not occur.

The reef structure itself benefits all the reef's denizens, including those that forged it, by passively trapping nutrients carried to the sea in stream waters. These streams, flowing into the lagoons behind the reefs, convey nutrients that would be diluted by the vast open seas were the reefs not effective at trapping their precious cargo.

Because tropical forests are often very effective at retaining soil nutrients, the streams that drain undisturbed tropical watersheds can have lower nutrient concentrations than does the rain. Under those circumstances, the ability of reefs to trap stream nutrients in lagoons is particularly important. Unfortunately, in situations where forest disturbance causes streams to convey nutrient-rich water to the lagoons, the same ability can result in the death of the reef.

Relations among the fish inhabiting coral reefs are complex. Some fish clean the skin, gills, and teeth of other fish. Others school in dense formations that resemble larger fish. Mary Gleason, while a graduate student at the University of California, Berkeley, observed coral with and without the territorial damselfish present; she found that these small fish, which hide out among the nooks and crannies of the reef top, enhance the health of reefs by harassing the crown-of-thorns starfish and other coral predators.

Coral reefs abound in mysteries. Many details of the animal-algae symbiosis are not understood, such as how the individual algal cells invade new coral polyps. Another mystery concerns the overall productivity of healthy reefs, which, acre for acre, is exceeded by no other ecosystem on the planet. The seawaters that wash over reefs are generally so nutrient-poor that it is hard to understand how reefs can be as productive as they are. Although cultivation of algae by coral and the architecture of reefs do help conserve and trap nutrients within the reef, some scientists do not believe this is sufficient to explain the fertility of reefs. Phosphorus (an essential ingredient in ATP, the substance that allows living cells to store and utilize energy) is so scarce in seawater that this nutrient ought to limit the growth of reefs. Reef productivity is puzzling in the same way as would be a village that thrives solely on tourism even though the tourists bring virtually no money; no matter how thrifty the people, an inflow of resources is needed to sustain wealth.

An insightful observation by the late John Isaacs, an oceanographer at the Scripps Marine Laboratory in San Diego, sheds some light on this puzzle.[1] Why, he asked, are there no "pelagic trees"? A pelagic tree would be a tree growing in the open waters of the sea (called the pelagic zone). He did not mean trees, literally, but rather organisms like trees that have both roots with which to draw up nutrients and a canopy for purposes of gathering light. In deep-sea water, such an organism would have to be quite tall, of course, for the deep waters of the sea are nutrient-rich while the sunlight only penetrates the surface waters. But if pelagic trees existed, they would grow magnificently. Just like coral reef organisms. Observations of that sort are often the stimulus for new ideas in science.

By looking at the world in a novel way and asking why something does not exist, one often triggers new and useful thoughts. Based on the observation that there are no pelagic trees, two other marine scientists proposed that reefs must benefit from deep ocean nutrients.[2] To understand their proposal, called the endo-upwelling concept, let us return to South Florida for a moment and take another look at the Florida aquifer, the same underground reservoir of water that played a role in stopping the jetport planned there.

1. J. Isaacs, "The Nature of Oceanic Life," *Scientific American* 221 (September 1969):146–162.

2. F. Rougerie and B. Wauthy, "The Endo-Upwelling Concept: A New Paradigm for Solving an Old Paradox," Proceedings of the Sixth International Coral Reef Symposium 3:21–26, edited by J. Choat et al., Townsville, Australia, 1988.

A mile or so below the everglades, a subterranean "hot plate" creates a mass of slowly rising hot aquifer water. The Florida aquifer comes in contact with the heated crust of the earth, and this heat forces aquifer water to rise through the porous limestone. According to the endo-upwelling concept (which not all oceanographers accept), a similar mechanism nourishes reefs: deep nutrient-rich water, forced upward by geothermal heat, penetrates slowly through the porous atolls and brings nutrients to the reef organisms at the surface.

And so it seems that coral reefs are organized to thrive: they are assemblages of life geared to make more and more life the way Bartholomew Cubbins made hats. But all is not as harmonious as it seems. Deep beneath the living crown of the reef, beneath the spectacular profusion of color, form, and symbiotic function, there lies embedded in the coralline bedrock a silent record of a historical drama played out between sea and sky. As with all insightful history, this record may, as we shall see, tell us not only about the history of reefs but about their fate as well.

In winter 1983, strong winds and intense rainfall clobbered the coast of California. Flooding occurred up and down the coast, while huge landslides closed off sections of the coastal roadways. It was one of the wettest California winters in the past century. Around the world, people experienced different but equally unusual conditions. From Tahiti to Indonesia, sea level dropped abnormally. Tahiti experienced one of the severer cyclones in its history. In Indonesia and Central America, drought conditions prevailed. The Galápagos Islands received about ten times the normal amount of rain that year. And fish inhabiting the waters off the coast of Peru were probably hungry that winter, for 1983 was an El Niño year.

El Niño means "the child" in Spanish. This name was conferred by Peruvian fishermen because the first signal of this climatic and climactic event often occurs around Christmastime along the coast of Peru. The signal that the fishermen first notice is an unusual warming of the seawater. In years when this warming is particularly intense, like 1983, it often means hard times for the fishermen, not because of the warming itself but because of the source of the warming.

In normal years (recently designated "La Niña" years), there is intense upwelling of deep water off the South American coast, bringing deep, cool water to the surface. This deep water is a rich source of nourishment for life in the coastal waters because it contains the nutrients released from the sunken corpses of marine plankton. In El Niño years, the upwelling of deep, cold, nutrient-rich water virtually ceases, thus increasing the temperature of the surface water and causing the fish to suffer a scarcity of nutrients.

What alters the upwelling every so often? The answer is a little like the kind of reply you sometimes get when you ask what causes the stock market to drop now and then—loss of investor confidence brought about by excessive rise in stock prices. Then when you ask why stocks recover, the answer is often that prices are low and investors see great bargains in front of them. In other words, there are cyclical forces at work. Like the stock market-investor system, the coupled ocean-atmosphere system contains many causal loops, or cyclical sequences of connected events. In rough outline, here is how El Niños and La Niñas alternate in time. The trade winds blow from east to west across the subtropical southern Pacific. These winds rub against the sea surface and cause surface ocean currents to flow the same way. The effect of this would be a piling up of water on the western edge of the Pacific, but of course water does not remain piled up in a mound. The tremendous weight of piled-up water pushes down on the water beneath it, creating a return flow of water, from west to east, below the sea surface. In normal years, then, this deeper and therefore colder water is forced upward as it encounters the South American coast, creating the relatively cool conditions usually found there. To understand El Niño, we next have to ask, what drives the winds that create this oceanic conveyor belt? Here is where the circularity of the system comes in, for the winds are themselves partly driven by sea surface temperatures.

In the equatorial zone, warm temperatures cause rising columns of heated air, some of which then flows north and some south at high elevation. At higher latitudes, this heated air descends over some of the major deserts of the world—those of the southwestern United States and Mexico as well as the Sahara in the north, and the deserts of Australia, southern Africa, and South America. It is no accident that the major deserts of the world lie in the bull's-eye of this descending air, for it is hot and dry, having had all the moisture wrung out of it in the form of tropical rains.

This downwelling creates high-pressure zones, particularly off the west coast of South America because cool seas chill the air there, while the warmer seas in the western tropical Pacific lead to lower air pressure. Since winds tend to blow from places with high pressure to those with low, that pressure difference helps sustain the east to west airflow. Moreover, as the descending air approaches earth's surface, it tends to flow toward the equator because the rising air created a vacuum. And at that point, it is deflected toward the west because of the earth's rotation.[3]

But as the upwelling water continues to cool the coastal waters of South America, it also increasingly cools off the air above that region, eventually weakening the rising equatorial airflow. This means weakened equatorward flow of air and reduced pressure difference between the eastern and western Pacific. Thus, the trade winds weaken, and less water is pushed westward. As a result, sea level in the central and western Pacific drops, slowing the eastward push of deep water and its upwelling off the west coast of South America. The atmosphere-ocean system is then in its El Niño phase. La Niña years return when the warm seas of the eastern Pacific, the result of diminished cold-water upwelling in El Niño years, regenerate strong updrafts and hence strong trade winds.

To summarize this jumble of puzzle pieces, let us look at the big picture. Trade winds push surface water to the west, thereby creating a return flow of deeper cooler water that cools the air. As that cooling of the air slows the trade winds, the upwelling of cool water also slows, and the air begins to warm. That warming creates a vertical updraft that jump starts the trade winds—a perfect setup for a system that keeps shutting off and on, or that oscillates, as scientists would say.

Now we can see why El Niño years are likely to be characterized by the weather patterns described earlier. During El Niño years, the warmer air in the eastern Pacific causes more evaporation, and that must mean more rain somewhere. Why California and the Galápagos Islands but not Central America? Hard to say. And, in fact, not all

3. To see why, picture yourself on a stream of air moving toward the equator from the Northern Hemisphere. The air mass you travel on and the solid earth below you are both rotating toward the east, but as you travel south, you are going at a constant rate east, while the earth is not. Proceeding south, the easterly velocity of the earth below increases (imagine a spinning globe: for it to maintain a constant rotation rate, a spot on the equator has to turn faster than a spot farther north, because the former has farther to go in one rotation). Thus, the earth appears to move away from you toward the east as you move toward the equator. Looked at from the vantage point of an observer at a fixed location on the earth's surface rather than one traveling with the wind, the moving air mass is seen to be curving toward the west.

El Niño years correspond to wet years in California. Although 1983 was a very wet El Niño year in California, 1987 was a terribly dry El Niño year there.

When this interplay between sea and sky produces an El Niño event, biological havoc can result. In the Galápagos Islands, finches (the same species of finches whose beaks Darwin once studied and used as evidence of adaptation in nature) bred profusely in 1983, with some birds laying ten clutches and one female producing twenty-five young. Ornithologists Peter Grant and B. Rosemary Grant observed that some of the young were born, matured, and were ready to breed that same year. Alan Pounds, a scientist at the Monteverde Cloud Forest Reserve in Costa Rica, speculates that the rare and beautiful golden toad disappeared from that reserve in 1987 because of a drought caused by an El Niño event that year. The toad requires wet burrows to survive the dry season; the unusually dry conditions of 1987 may have caused these burrows to become inhospitable.

In Kalimantan, Indonesia, the severe drought helped turn what might have been a routine forest fire into the largest forest fire in recorded history anywhere, destroying up to half the forest and wildlife in an area of over two million square miles. It is nearly certain that the fire was deliberately set by people wanting to clear land for agriculture and settlement. This "slash and burn" (or swidden) style of agriculture can be a perfectly sustainable way to prepare forested land for farming, provided it is carried out in a rotation scheme in which the land has time to recover periodically and the amount of cleared land is not increased each year (and, of course, provided it does not lead to a conflagration because of widespread drought). In societies in which population size did not change much, held in check by one means or another, this method of agriculture was a sensible adaptation to tropical or semitropical conditions. But in Indonesia, vast new areas of forest in Kalimantan are being cleared to resettle the growing population of Java, in some cases without the willing consent of the settlers.

The species loss from the Kalimantan fire is inestimable and the prospects for recovery of the forest uncertain but grim. Measured solely in terms of how much carbon dioxide this one fire emitted to the atmosphere, the damage was high. A reasonable estimate is that nearly two billion tons of this climate-altering gas entered the atmosphere as a result of the fire, an amount equal to that produced from one month of fossil fuel burning at current world consumption rates.

El Niño events can damage coral reefs in a variety of ways. Lowered sea levels in the central and western Pacific cause damage because the organisms inhabiting coral reefs cannot tolerate prolonged exposure to the air. Intense oceanic storms in the central Pacific often accompany the sea level depression, causing further stress to reefs as strong wave action from each storm physically damages the reef architecture. The 1983 cyclone in Tahiti, for example, caused extensive damage to the already stressed reefs of those islands. The warmer sea surface temperatures that accompany El Niño events in the eastern Pacific can also damage coral, as was observed by marine biologists from the Gulf of Panama to the Galápagos Islands during the 1983 El Niño. The damage was patchy, however, suggesting that there may have been variations in the rate and amount of temperature rise and/or variations in the susceptibility of coral to that rise.

By drilling into a coral reef, beyond the living surface and down into the ancient dead coral bed beneath, a core of coral can be extracted. Probing into a reef is tantamount to going back in time. Examined closely, cores from Indonesian reefs reveal a series of closely spaced, dark bands of varying thickness. Like growth rings in trees, these bands tell us something about yearly events in the life of the coral. The dark bands, it turns out, contain fulvic acid—a common constituent of the partially decomposed organic matter found in soils. In La Niña years, rain falling on the land surface near the reefs erodes soil, and some of this eroded material is washed out to sea where it can be deposited right on the reef. During El Niño years, however, storms in Indonesia are weaker and rarer than in normal years, so less erosion occurs and the bands are paler.[4] Evidence of this sort tells us that El Niños are not just a recent phenomenon. Life has had to adapt to the environmental stress of El Niños during the past millennium at least, quite likely for much longer than that.

The record of natural soil erosion revealed in coral cores, such as in La Niña years in Indonesia, is also of intrinsic interest. If the erosion is not too severe, reefs are well adapted to this phenomenon and indeed benefit from the nutrient in the eroded soil. If it were not for human disturbance, most of today's living reefs would probably live for five or

4. Michael Moore, a graduate student in geography at the University of California, Berkeley, has been doing some of the best work of this type in Indonesia. His recent findings suggest that the fulvic acid technique may have to be supplemented with another method, based on analysis of variations in the trace amounts of nuclear isotopes in the reef core, to get reliable reconstructions of past El Niños.

ten more millennia before succumbing either to suffocation from too much sediment deposited on the reef or to air exposure from falling seas that will occur when the next ice age sets in (because a large volume of seawater will be locked up in glacial ice). As we shall see, human disturbance could greatly shorten their lives.

Below the steep and jagged peaks of Mo'orea in French Polynesia lies some of the most fertile soil in the world—a chocolate brown, organically rich treasure that looks and smells good enough to eat. The mixture of clay, which holds in reserve the essential mineral elements for plant growth,[5] and sand, which drains away the torrential rains that frequently occur, is ideal for pineapple, taro, papaya, and the other crops that grow profusely wherever the native vegetation is cleared. Offshore, on the edge of the lagoon that fringes the island, lies another treasure—an abundance of delicious reef fish, available for netting or spearing.

Such is the ideal, the Gauguin vision of tropical paradise. But the reality is sadly askew. After a heavy rainstorm in November 1990, I climbed a ridge high above Pao Pao Bay, on Mo'orea, to witness a ghastly sight. Where just the day before the crystalline waters of the bay hosted a gathering of spinner dolphins in for a rest from their nightly fishing expedition farther out to sea, now there was a huge murky brown clot of earthy water slowly moving out of the bay toward the reef and open sea. It was easy to see that the immediate source of the soil entering the bay was a single stream that drained the valley between two large mountains.

The valley is intensively farmed, primarily for pineapple. Mature pineapple plants are about two feet tall. They grow best in well-tilled soil, in rows a few feet apart. Seen from above, from a raindrop's viewpoint, the pineapple plantations are a mix of about one part green—the pineapple plants—and two parts brown—the bare and well-tilled soil. Intense storms wash away the loose soil, and streams carry it out to the coastal waters. In some parts of Mo'orea, such as the Opunohu val-

5. These minerals include calcium, potassium, sodium, and magnesium. They are held in chemical bondage within the lattice of the clay, released on demand by plants but not readily dissolved out of the clay unless the rain is acidic.

ley, the soil is less intensively farmed. There, the streams should not be silting up so much in the aftermath of torrential rains, and the reefs offshore from this bay should be less threatened by siltation and over-fertilization.

This lush, pristine valley, one of the few in the Tahitian islands that has been spared from the plow, may be converted into a golf course and resort by Japanese developers. Tahitian authorities gave tentative permission in 1991 for the destruction of one of the last remaining wild places on the island despite the protests of numerous environmental groups. Apparently, land is so expensive in Japan that it is cheaper to develop a golf course in Tahiti and fly the golfers there than it is to build it in Japan. Local environmentalists are vigorously opposing this development; as of this writing, it appears they will be successful.

In 1990, Michael Poole, then a graduate student from the University of California, Santa Cruz, studying the behavior of the spinner dolphins in Mo'orea, became concerned about the effects of siltation of coastal waters on his subjects as well as on the reefs that surround the island. He and I have now begun a study that we hope will shed light on the interaction between land use and the health of coral reefs. By contrasting the amount of eroded soil flushing out onto the reef at the mouth of Pao Bay with the amount at the mouth of Opunohu Bay, and at the same time surveying the health of the reefs bathed by these bay waters, we have what is, in effect, a nicely controlled experiment. Of course, if the Japanese resort is built, then the Opunohu valley will no longer be the pristine control system that it now is; erosion will occur from the construction of the resort, and a scientific opportunity, as well as a beautiful valley, will be lost.

Erosion from agriculture, dredging, road building, clear-cutting, and other human activities is probably the major cause of reef degradation throughout the tropical world today, although few studies have actually demonstrated the connection. In one of the best studies to date, a doctoral dissertation by University of Hawaii student George Hodgson, it was shown that erosion from the building of roads used to haul timber out of the clear-cut forests in the Philippines is causing extensive siltation of reef waters and damage to coral. In Australia, massive soil erosion onto the Great Barrier Reef has been shown to be triggered by construction of a roadway in the forest along the coast of northern Queensland, although it has proven difficult to assign a precise share of blame for reef damage there to this erosion. Charles Darwin may have been the first to raise the issue, having observed that reef development was limited in areas receiving excessive sediments from rivers flowing to the sea.[6]

Overfertilization and siltation from anthropogenic erosion are probably the major causes of reef damage today, with overfishing a close runner-up. But the future is likely to see more intense damage from a different source and on an even larger geographic scale. This damage will result from global warming, and to understand how climate change might affect reefs, it helps to swing back in time.

Sixty million years ago, Australia was not as close to the equator as it now is. Since then, the Australian tectonic plate has been slowly moving northward toward the equator, causing the climate of Australia to warm gradually. Even a mere twenty million years ago, water temperatures off the coast of that continent were too cool for coral to grow. As Australia moved north, subtropical ocean currents flowing westward from the mid-Pacific were deflected southward from its northeastern tip, which then caused further warming along the eastern coast. By fifteen million years ago, the seawater off the northeastern tip should have been warm enough for coral to thrive, while a couple of million years ago, coral should have been able to grow near what is today the southern tip of the Great Barrier Reef.

Sure enough, when the deep, ancient beds of dead coral beneath the present living crown of the Great Barrier Reef were recently cored and dated, the most northerly part of the old reef was found to be about fifteen million years old and three to four thousand feet thick. And the southern limit of today's reef sits on a dead coral bed only two to three million years old and four to five hundred feet thick.

Coral has both lower and upper temperature limits. Generally, once water temperatures exceed 85 degrees Fahrenheit, corals bleach and eventually die after prolonged exposure. It is the algae living within the coral that apparently are most sensitive to high temperatures, and it is their death that results in the bleached appearance of the coral. The five- to ten-degree warming of eastern Pacific waters that accompanies El Niño events has been observed to damage corals at sites scattered along the coast of equatorial South America and as far north as the Gulf of Panama. But that is a perfectly natural occurrence to which corals have been exposed for millennia. Of greater concern is the impending global warming from the buildup of greenhouse gases in our atmo-

6. Charles Darwin, 1851, *The Structure and Distribution of Coral Reefs* (Berkeley and Los Angeles: University of California Press, reprint ed., 1962).

sphere. This warming is projected to raise seawater temperatures in the tropics by 1 to 4 degrees Fahrenheit during the next fifty years. Some of the planet's living coral will still be bathed in water below the 85-degree critical value when this occurs, but not all of it will, and widespread damage is expected. And, of course, when the average temperature of the sea is raised, El Niños will do greater damage as more tropical American reefs are pushed over the critical temperature limit.

In 1991, an unusually severe coral bleaching episode erupted in the reefs surrounding the island of Mo'orea. Rising water temperature was observed then as well, but its cause is unknown; perhaps it was an early symptom of global warming or just a fluctuation resulting from the El Niño event that year. If the latter is true, the bleaching event was part of the natural course (like gap formation in a forest), to which life in coral reefs has adapted through the millennia. If the former is correct, however, then another fuse has blown, with effects that will accumulate over time and lead to a catastrophic loss of biodiversity.

Global warming could also damage coral reefs by inundating them under rising seas. Again, let us look to the past for insight. Twenty thousand years ago, during the last ice age, so much seawater was locked up in glacial ice that sea levels were nearly five hundred feet lower than they are today. Hence, the currently living reefs of the world could not have existed then. They would have been high and dry. The living crown of the Great Barrier Reef today is only about one thousand years old. During this time, the sea level there has varied because of natural causes by only two or three inches per century, while the Caribbean reefs have experienced a sea level rise on the order of six inches per century. Interestingly, the Caribbean reefs have also been accumulating limestone at a rate faster than others around the world, thus keeping pace with the rapidly rising seas there.

At maximum productivity, corals can produce two and a half pounds of limestone per year on each square foot of reef, corresponding to a maximum of four-tenths of an inch of growth per year on the coral bed. Thus, most reefs will not be able to keep up with sea level rise from global warming if the higher projections of four feet or more during the next century are correct. Unfortunately, we know very little about the effect on the species composition and productivity of the top of a living reef when it is under a foot or two more water.

Regardless of what sea level rise from global warming does to reefs, that rise will not go unnoticed in the tropical Pacific. Some very low, flat island nations will lose substantial portions of their territory if seas rise a mere foot or two. Saltwater intrusion, the same mechanism that we saw destroys underground freshwater supplies in South Florida when swamps are drained, is likely to jeopardize the freshwater supplies of many island nations. Here, rising seas will force salt water into the underground "lenses" of drinking water that sit beneath their land.

While I watched the mud skippers at Pulau Dua, an unmistakable rich, pungent odor of decay, tinged with a hint of rotten eggs, emanated from the surrounding mud flats. The odor brought to mind yet another set of threats to coral reefs around the world. A lengthy detour will explain why.

That odor characteristic of mud flats means that the oxygen content of the muck is low, a result of oxygen consumption by the microorganisms decomposing organic matter there. Shallow coastal waters around the world are often in a similar condition, especially if human sewage is discharged into the waters, but also under perfectly natural conditions.

If you were to place a jar open-end down, just a little bit into the mud, and collect for a few minutes the rising gas bubbles, there would be some nitrous oxide in the jar, along with carbon dioxide, hydrogen sulfide, and other emanations from the rotting muck. Nitrous oxide is odorless and colorless. It is produced by microorganisms who earn a living converting nitrate[7] into either molecular nitrogen or nitrous oxide, in a process called denitrification. It is a perfectly natural process, although it can be accelerated by overuse of nitrate fertilizers on farmland. We shall see that the microbes, known as denitrifying bacteria, play a major role in determining the fitness of the biosphere for all forms of life.

Nitrous oxide is so unreactive, chemically, that it does not break down or combine with other gases in the lower atmosphere. Slowly but surely it makes its way to the stratosphere, the layer of the atmosphere above about eight miles, where supersonic aircraft fly. In the

7. Readers may recall from chapter 1 that nitrate, like ammonia, is a form of nitrogen that plants can use for their nitrogen requirements. Nitrate is rich in oxygen compared to nitrous oxide, so the conversion of nitrate to nitrous oxide or to nitrogen can occur in waters or soil low in freely available oxygen, and indeed it is in such places that the reaction is often most vigorous.

stratosphere, it finally reacts[8] and breaks apart. At this stage, a seemingly implausible link between microorganisms underfoot and the stratospheric ozone shield overhead is joined. To understand this link, let us look at the dynamics of stratospheric ozone.

Ozone in the stratosphere is a gas to which we all owe thanks, for without it, a lethal rain of ultraviolet (UV) radiation from the sun would destroy nearly all of life on earth. Ozone is produced in the stratosphere when high-energy packets or quanta of sunlight strike ordinary oxygen molecules in the stratosphere, splitting these molecules into two oxygen atoms; one of the atoms (O) then combines with molecular oxygen (O_2) to produce ozone (O_3)—a molecule consisting of three oxygen atoms.[9] If that were the end of it and nothing destroyed the ozone, then ozone production would continue until all the molecular oxygen in the stratosphere was converted to ozone. And for the evolution of life on earth, that would have been almost as bad news as too little ozone, for virtually no mutation-causing UV radiation would have penetrated to the earth's surface. Mutations are often associated with monsters and cancer, but they are also the primary cause of genetic variation among organisms, which, in turn, is a driving force behind the evolution of all the life forms on the planet.

Now back to the broken-down nitrous oxide in the stratosphere. One of the products of its demise is nitric oxide, a gas that triggers a pair of chemical reactions leading to the disintegration of ozone. It is this process that keeps the ozone level in the stratosphere in a balance between too little (which would shower us all with harmful radiation) and too much (which would reduce mutation rates and slow evolutionary change). Ultimately, then, it is the lowly denitrifying bacteria, chomping away on nitrate in the smelly mud flats and the soils around

8. Most nitrous oxide molecules (N_2O is the molecular formula) are struck by high-energy quanta of sunlight in the stratosphere and break apart into a nitrogen molecule (N_2) and an atom of oxygen (O). But about 1 percent of the nitrous oxide molecules react with atomic oxygen to form two molecules of nitric oxide (NO). It is the nitric oxide by-product of nitrous oxide that initiates the destruction of stratospheric ozone.

9. The reason ozone is created high in the atmosphere by this mechanism, in the region called the stratosphere, and not in the lower atmosphere, the troposphere, is that the high-energy quanta of sunlight do not penetrate to the lower atmosphere because they are nearly all absorbed in the stratosphere. In the troposphere, ozone is created by a different process, and there it is a health hazard, not a blessing. It is created in urban air from hydrocarbons and oxides of nitrogen, emitted largely by automobiles, when those pollutants mix in the presence of sunlight. A major component of smog, ozone causes respiratory damage to people and can also damage vegetation.

the globe, that determine how much mutation-causing UV radiation we receive.

In the 1970s, a few scientists voiced concern that the excess nitrate entering soils, streams, and estuaries as fertilizer runoff from farmland would increase the rate of denitrification, thereby increasing the flow of nitrous oxide to the stratosphere and causing the level of ozone in the stratosphere to decline.[10] This concern is still a serious one and someday will surely be headline news as our overnitrified planet increasingly denitrifies, further thinning the ozone layer and increasing UV radiation at the earth's surface. But the urgency of this threat has recently been overshadowed by a related, but more immediate, threat to the stratospheric ozone layer.

In the mid-1980s, evidence accumulated showing that the ozone layer was thinning above the antarctic from September through November. Soon thereafter, the cause became apparent; it involved not nitrous oxide but a collection of gases called chlorofluorocarbons (CFCs).[11] Like nitrous oxide, the CFCs rise inert through the lower atmosphere to the stratosphere, where they are broken down into a product (chlorine in this case) that starts the chemical reaction that destroys ozone. Unlike nitrous oxide, the CFCs are only produced industrially, not by bacteria in soil and water. The CFCs have many applications for human use, including refrigerants in automobile air-conditioners, foaming agents to create insulated packing material, cleansers in the electronics industries, and propellants in spray cans (a use that is virtually eliminated in the United States but occurs elsewhere).

Just a few years after it was first discovered, the hole in the antarctic ozone layer was found to be big enough to warrant immediate action. In 1987, many nations meeting in Montreal formally agreed to gradually reduce the use of CFCs. In early 1989, with the problem looking even more serious, the European nations and the United States met again and agreed on the complete elimination of CFC production and use by the turn of the century. Although not all nations have signed the international agreements, the major producers and users of these

10. Harold Johnston, a chemistry professor at the University of California, Berkeley, first shed light on much of the science of the preceding paragraphs and played a key role in warning the public about the hazard of excess oxides of nitrogen in the stratosphere.

11. Two scientists, Mario Molino and Sherwood Rowland at the University of California, Irvine, had figured out a decade earlier that CFCs had the ability to destroy ozone and, like Johnston, warned the public of the menace.

destructive gases have, and the prospects are good that production and use will be virtually eliminated in a decade or less. Unfortunately, closing the CFC pipeline to the atmosphere will not immediately stop the ozone loss, because the CFCs emitted over the past several decades will continue to destroy ozone well into the next century. As a result, further ozone thinning and increased UV radiation are expected.

We know already that the problem is no longer confined to the antarctic, where it was first discovered. Over the midlatitudes of the Northern Hemisphere, the ozone layer has thinned by about 3 percent during the past decade, less than the thinning in the antarctic but enough to cause around half a million new cataracts and a hundred thousand new cases of skin cancer worldwide each year because of increased UV radiation. While nearly all these skin cancers are treatable, several thousand new cases per year of melanoma, a much more serious cancer that is fatal in about 25 percent of the cases, are also predicted.

What does the ozone problem have to do with coral reefs? Aren't they protected underwater? Unfortunately, the few feet of seawater above life in the shallow seas offers little protection from UV radiation, for the clear waters of reefs are fairly transparent to this radiation, down to depths of tens of feet. Tropical UV radiation is projected to increase by up to 10 percent over the next few decades, even with the international agreements in force (the increase would be far greater with no agreements). What will this do to life in the coral reefs? The sorry fact is we do not really know. Some minute forms of marine life, the plankton, are known to be very sensitive to even smaller increases in UV radiation than those predicted, and it is virtually certain that mortality of some individual organisms will increase as a result of higher radiation levels. It is less clear whether that will lead to systemwide effects, such as an overall decline in reef productivity. Speculation exists that it could lead to the outright extinction of some organisms, perhaps including participants in one of the many symbioses discussed earlier, which would, of course, mean dragging down other organisms as well.

Living coral reefs occupy but a tiny fraction of the ocean, yet within them lies a treasure trove of biodiversity. The marine environment, in general, and coral reefs, in particular, are unusual in that, compared to terrestrial environments, they contain a much higher amount of taxonomic diversity at the phylum level and other inclusive levels in the classification hierarchy. In terms of numbers of species, marine habitats contain less than 15 percent of the world's life forms; most of the species on earth are terrestrial insects, all belonging to only one of the many classes. But the oceans contain about two-thirds of all the phyla and classes. This means they contain two-thirds of all the highly and broadly distinct types of life. And within the oceans, most of that diversity is found in the coral reefs. Only about 1 percent of all marine taxa are found in the vast, open, deep waters of the oceans.

If reefs degrade, we could lose all the organisms in some of the higher levels of the taxonomic hierarchy. The extinction of an entire class or phylum is a much more serious loss than the loss of the same number of species in a much larger class or phylum that continues to exist. The reason biologists consider it to be more serious is that we are interested in the quality as well as the quantity of the information in the genetic "library" of life. Species in distinct phyla or classes differ much more dramatically from one another with respect to biochemistry, strategies of adaptation, and so forth, than do species within the same class or phylum. Loss of a class or phylum is like loss of all artworks in a unique historical period; loss of the same number of paintings representing all the periods in art history would certainly be a loss but not as great a loss.

The reefs of Tahiti contain fewer species than the reefs of Fiji to the west; the reefs of Australia are richer still in species, while those of the Philippines farther to the west contain the most diverse collection of species of any reefs in the world. The reason has to do with the west-blowing trade winds, those key actors in the El Niño cycle. These winds cause the equatorial ocean currents at the sea surface to also flow from east to west, and thus the natural trajectory of drifting organisms in the equatorial waters is from east to west. This replenishes the populations in the west and maintains their diversity at a higher level than in the east, much as we saw in chapter 5 how periodic movement of organisms to the tropics during ice ages maintains higher species diversity in the tropics than in the higher latitudes.

Cultural diversity of *Homo sapiens,* like that of wild species, is remarkably rich in the tropics. Linguists estimate that over one-third of the world's languages are spoken in the South Pacific islands. Very likely, a process similar to that by which species diversity became enriched in the waters around these islands is responsible: isolation interrupted by occasional cultural transplantations. But the interruptions have increased in recent years, to the point where they threaten to destroy rather than enhance this diversity (and that of the wild species as well). And thus I am reminded of Bill.

As a Fijian youngster growing up on a small islet off the island of Taveuni, Bill and his playmates would catch venomous sea snakes and drape them around their necks, pretending the shiny black and white banded creatures were jewelry. Years later, Bill learned from tourists, armed with facts and fears, how close to death they played.

When Bill was a teenager, in the 1950s, his family, along with the extended family that comprised his village, left their islet home and settled on Taveuni. He explained to me, as I accompanied him on a return visit to the islet, that the mud flats and waters surrounding their old home had once provided adequate food for the small tribe. But as their numbers grew and as they sought cash income, a move to Taveuni, with more arable land, became irresistible.

Bill often carries a long, light spear—a cluster of sharp metal prongs on a ten-foot bamboo pole. Seeing it continually unused, I had begun to wonder if its purpose was more mnemonic than predatory. One afternoon, however, as we were preparing to return to Taveuni after visiting his ancestral island, my doubts were erased. Bill was starting the outboard motor on his skiff while recounting some tribal history. I must have blinked when he threw the spear, because the next thing I saw was a quivering pole impaled in the side of a frantic fish. He had hit a two-foot-long, black, fast-swimming trevally at a distance of fifty feet!

Earlier that day, he demonstrated how to catch stomatopods, lobsters with a menacing talon in their front claws used to impale and clasp their prey. The species on Fiji grow about a foot long and inhabit mud flats. At low tide, their burrow openings are easy to spot at the edge of the sea, but the trick is to get them out of the burrows, which extend down a foot or so and then back as much as ten feet toward open water. Bill rammed a heavy, sharp stick into the mud ten feet seaward of the opening, wiggled it, and asked if I saw anything peculiar at the burrow opening ten feet away. I did not, so he moved down the coast a few feet and tried again. This time I saw undulating water at the burrow hole. He moved a foot or so closer to the opening and again rammed the stick in. This time water burbled even more emphatically at the opening. Gradually he worked the creature toward the daylight end of its burrow, until it was within a pace of the opening. A plunge with his spear, followed by an arm's-length grab into the burrow, and he had caught dinner.[12] This last step requires nerve and skill, because even when the spear hits home, the formidable pincers can still function.

Today, a single village contains most of the former inhabitants of Bill's childhood island home. They raise a variety of cash crops and grow most of their own fruits and vegetables. But Bill does not live in the village. His family and several of his close relatives own land on a hillside about ten miles away. Bill and I walked one day along most of the trails that snake through their nearly 250 acres, from the coast to the dividing ridge down the center of Taveuni. Much of the land is covered with old-growth forest, but here and there are small clearings planted with coconut palm, papaya, taro, kava,[13] and other crops.

On this walk, the full cause, extent, and implications of Bill's ambitions became clear. Indians on Fiji now outnumber native Fijians by a small margin. They are also the more entrepreneurial and own most of the businesses and tourist facilities. Many Fijians, including Bill, resent this. Along with his wife and daughter, he worked for many years at an expensive Taveuni resort run by an Indian. Pay was meager and the workday long. Worse yet, it was demeaning for Bill in a way that even subsistence living would not be. When Bill and his family announced they were quitting, in 1988, the boss told him he would be crawling back starving in six months.

12. Although I enjoyed dinner that evening, I might not have if I had known then what I learned about a month later from Rick Steger, a marine biologist who was studying stomatopods at the University of California's R. C. Gump Marine Biological Station on the French Polynesian island of Mo'orea. While many stomatopod mysteries remain, these feisty little hook-clawed lobsters *are* known to do something that is quite rare in the animal kingdom: they mate for life. Well, almost. It turns out that even they make exceptions. A single male and female, plus any youngsters, live together in each burrow, and it is the male's responsibility to sally forth to the sea in search of food for the family. Occasionally, however, he ends up as dinner for a shark or a person, or whatever. And in that event, a neighboring male may just abandon his own mate and burrow up with the widow. It appears that this will only occur, however, if the widow is larger than the current mate.

13. Kava root is boiled to prepare a frequently and ritually drunk soupy tea. It is nonalcoholic but induces a sleepy, tingly euphoria. Kava is a kind of currency among Fijians and their guests as well. Visitors bring it as a gift much the way Westerners bring flowers or wine to dinner parties; in Fiji, it is considered offensive to show up at a village without some.

A year later, Bill had created on his land, down by the waterfront, a beautiful and ecologically nonobtrusive campground for low-budget travelers. His wife, a talented dancer and organizer of the village dance troop, is also a superb cook and prepares delicious Fijian meals for the campers. They keep the campsite immaculately clean, and to top it off, Bill's knowledge of where rare birds, such as the silktail and the orange dove, lurk on Taveuni is at the service of his guests.

The campsite is only a first step beyond "crawling" in Bill's mind, however. Bill wants to show the Indians of Fiji that he can do better than they. In that game, sadly, better means bigger. As we strode over his land, he showed me his planned site for a future resort for the wealthy, right on the ridge top with commanding views of both the east and west coast waters. And midway down the slope he had another development planned to accommodate middle-income tourists.

Road access will be needed, where now only trails lace the forested slope. Construction of roads and buildings will surely cause erosion in the rainy season. The splendid coral reef that lies just one hundred feet offshore from Bill's coastal campground will suffer as eroding soil spills into the sea. Tourism will probably boom, as the initially lush forests, diverse reef life, and exotic birds attract tourists, and then bust, as the ecological damage eventually sends the tourists off to other less-spoiled South Pacific islands, if any are left. Like the stomatopod, Bill and his island paradise are being driven toward destruction.

On one rainy night on Pulau Dua, we slept in the coral lean-to. In our mummy bags with their gaudy, Day-Glo-colored nylon cases, all snug within the limestone chamber of the lean-to, we might have looked a little like a gigantically magnified fragment of the living reef that once fringed Pulau Dua.

That image does not do justice, however, to the true extent to which humanity is a component of coral reefs. Whole nations are built on the skeletons of once-thriving reefs. Many tens of millions of people derive a substantial amount of their protein from the fish attracted to healthy coral reefs. Tourists spend large sums of money for the privilege of a few days of snorkeling or diving in reefs. Mysteries of coral reef ecology will grip the curiosity of scientists as long as reefs and science exist. And to those who never study, visit, eat the products of, or live on, reefs, the gift is no less desirable; like reception of a card announcing that a distant relative gave birth to a healthy child, knowledge that healthy reefs exist is a reminder of the perfection and the mystery of life.

And what is humanity's gift in return to these splendid living treasures? To date it is overfishing, siltation and overfertilization from erosion on mismanaged land, enhanced UV radiation because of our destruction of the stratospheric ozone layer, and the promise of slow cooking from global warming—a multitude of threats that jeopardize the health of coral reefs around the world.[14]

We could bear better gifts—gifts like family planning, wise management of marine and soil resources, use of substitutes for CFCs, energy conservation, and development of solar technologies. Much healthy reef remains, and our actions to date have by and large not led to irreversible damage. The burning fuse can still be doused.

14. Readers interested in a detailed look at the status of individual reefs around the world should consult the encyclopedic work, *Coral Reefs of the World,* 3 vols., edited by Susan Wells, United Nations Environmental Program Regional Seas Directories and Bibliographies (Nairobi, Kenya, and Gland, Switzerland: UNEP and IUCN, 1988).

7

THE SINISTER SIDE OF SYNERGY

The smudgy face that peered out through the yak-skin cloak gazed on a seemingly endless upsloping field of sparse grass and abundant rock. Looking to the right, the three-year-old child could see the snowcapped summit of Amnemachin, a 22,000-foot mountain that is sacred to his nomadic tribe. On the left roared the cascading milky waters of a tributary to the Yellow River, fed from glacial melt. The yak skin that engulfed both the child and the father who nestled him broke the bite of the harsh wind that seems never to cease on the Tibetan Plateau. Father and child bounced along on a yak, behind which ambled two other yaks—one carrying the child's mother, the other a few iron pots and their home, a yak-skin tent called a "yurt." Hefty eight-foot-long wooden poles accompanied the yurt, for no trees grow in this terrain. A rifle of World War II vintage was lashed to the crude saddlebag on the lead yak. This child's world—the vast windy space ahead, a mountain to the right, a river to the left, warmth behind, and a yak beneath—is like no other's.

The trio did not see me as I crouched on a cliff above and in fact probably saw no people for the next ten days and one hundred miles. They were setting out, alone, on a pilgrimage around the sacred mountain, traveling clockwise through the uninhabited land as required by the tenets of Buddhism. For me, the worn words "nuclear family unit" rang true for the first time.

Ngolog, pronounced go-log, is the name of their tribe. This Tibetan word means "people with their heads on backward," a name allegedly conferred on them by the ruling Tibetans to the south, who were frequently harassed by these stubborn and wild nomads who bloodily resisted the extension of Tibetan rule in the northern Tibetan Plateau. Culturally and linguistically, these nomads of Qinghai Province, China, are rather similar to the Buddhists of the former nation of Tibet, although politically their homeland has had a different history. Whereas Tibet existed as an independent nation in the twentieth century until Chinese subjugation and annexation in the 1950s, parts of Qinghai Province have been subjected to Chinese or Tibetan rule, on and off, since the early eighteenth century. Despite their history, the Ngologs' nomadic ways were relatively unaffected by whichever nation or warlord happened to claim their land. Even after 1957, when the Peoples' Liberation Army of China brought them under Communist rule, religious observances like the Amnemachin pilgrimage or placement of their dead on cliffs where the vultures can feast are still practiced by some Ngologs. In other ways, however, Communist domination has brought great changes to Qinghai Province.

Ngolog history, at least as recorded by Western explorers, is replete with colorful stories of their fierce resistance to domination or even foreign intrusion on their land. Some of the most brutally vivid accounts of how the Ngologs dealt with foreigners are recorded by the early explorers of the region, such as Alexandra David Neel who traveled through the Kunlun mountain range in the late nineteenth century. She and others who followed recount that traders and explorers who traveled the silk route to China and fell into the clutches of the Ngologs would be greeted with such welcoming rituals as being sewn inside a yak skin and thrown into the raging Yellow River.

This part of the world seems to encourage exaggeration and spawn myth, so we may never know the true nature of the pre-Communist Ngologs. The exaggerator par excellence was Leonard Clark, who wrote about Amnemachin in his journey narrative, *The Marching Wind*. Clark, a soldier of fortune from the United States, traveled to Amnemachin in the early 1940s looking for a place to which Chiang Kai-shek's army could retreat if the strengthening Communist forces proved to be too much for the Nationalists. His cockeyed scheme was

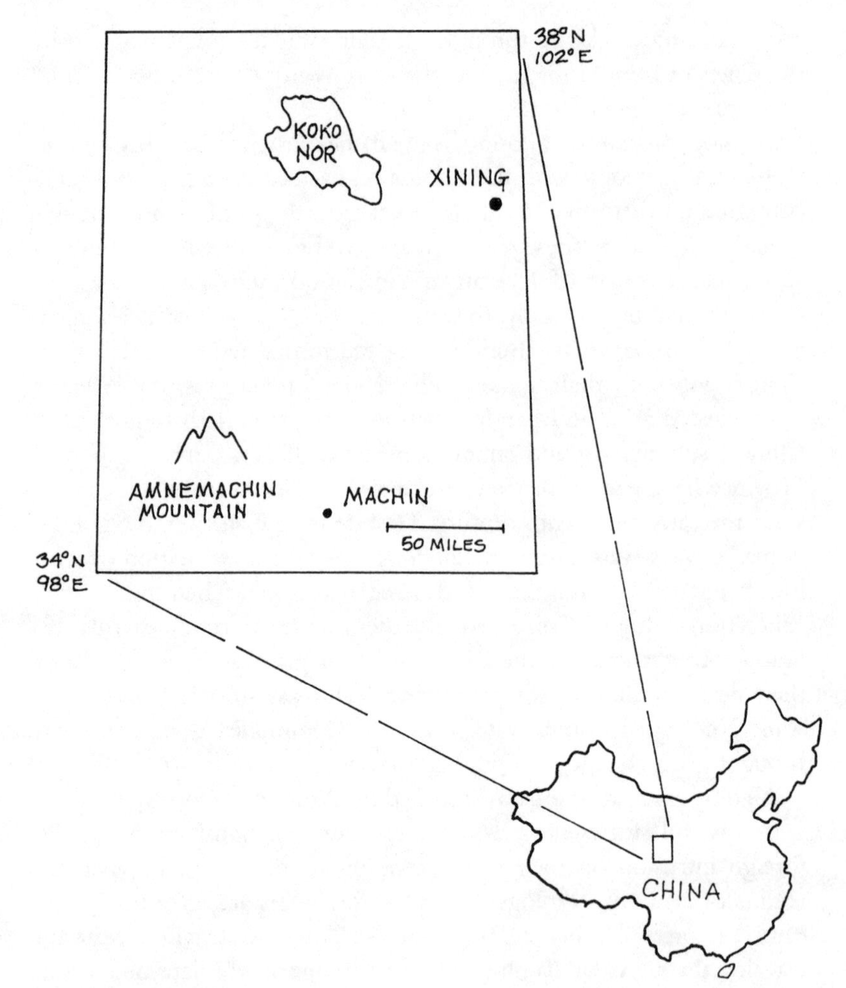

that the Nationalist forces would rebuild their strength in the Kunluns and then descend and sweep victoriously through China. Among his findings from the expedition, he claimed that Amnemachin was higher than Mount Everest, and he even displayed in *The Marching Wind* a bogus geometric calculation to prove his point. Tales of Ngolog torture and brutality pervade his book. And for good measure, he propagated the myth that any foreigner who glimpses the sacred summit of Amnemachin will die a hideous death shortly thereafter.

In one respect, Clark and other pre-Communist visitors to Qinghai may not have exaggerated. All the historic accounts of the region around Amnemachin portray the area as a wildlife paradise, a kind of

Chinese Serengeti. Snow leopards, blue sheep, bears, wolves, gazelle, and argali (a mountain sheep with massive horns) once roamed here in abundance. These reports deserve to be taken seriously because many of the explorers were trained naturalists, particularly Nikolai Przhevalsky, Joseph Rock, and Brooke Dolan. Przhevalsky was a Russian naturalist and army officer who explored the Tibetan Plateau in the 1880s,[1] Rock was a U.S. botanist who journeyed there in the 1920s and stayed on in Tibet for most of the rest of his life, and Dolan was a U.S. zoologist who studied wildlife in the plateau in the 1930s. In the time between Clark's visit in the 1940s and a 1981 expedition of which I was a member, the Communist regime allowed no Westerners to enter the region, nor did they conduct their own census of the area's wildlife. So no records exist of the pace of wildlife decimation during these four decades.

Yet decimation has surely occurred. Scattered pockets of wildlife remain but most of the populations are rapidly heading toward extinction. On the high slopes surrounding the summit of Amnemachin, usually above 16,000 feet elevation, we saw occasional, small, remaining clusters of the wild blue sheep. Little else, however, remains except for numerous marmots, other rodents, and a spectacular number of hawks, eagles, owls, and vultures feeding on the rodents. Two factors account for the near-extinction of wildlife. First, herds of domestic sheep have taken over much of the habitat that supported the once-large wild populations, forcing the wild animals to retreat to the narrow margins of higher land that lie between the domestic herds and the permanent snow line.

Second, the Ngologs we encountered took great pleasure and pride in hunting wild animals. Tibetan Buddhists are viewed by many in the West as nonviolent and respectful of nature, and perhaps they were before Chinese subjugation of the Tibetan Plateau. But we saw the Qinghai Buddhists as quite trigger-happy when it came to a tempting furry or feathered target. This was brought home to us at one point on our journey to Amnemachin when we came across a huge, bloated lamergeier (a type of vulture and one of the major beneficiaries when a Ngolog dies) waddling along feebly and unable to take off in flight because of an overstuffed stomach. Our Ngolog guide, a devout prac-

1. After Przhevalsky's death in 1888, while on an expedition in the Tibetan Plateau, the Russian czar gave his partner, V. I. Roberovsky, leadership of an exploring party. In 1895, Roberovsky had a paralytic seizure on the slope of Amnemachin, thereby helping to spawn the myth described above.

titioner of the Buddhist chants and circumambulations, immediately unslung his rifle and took aim. With wild gesticulations and loud protests, we managed to prevent this slaughter (although our later attempt to communicate to our guide with calmer hand motions the idea that one of his relatives might have been the cause of the overload was probably unsuccessful). Ben King, an ornithologist on the expedition, then picked up the bird, ran with it a few yards, and launched it in the air. It coasted for fifty yards, no more than ten feet from the ground, and then, to our delight, flapped its immense wings and ascended.

Love of hunting is not a recent phenomenon, for in the pre-sheep days on the plateau, wild animals were the only significant source of protein for the Ngologs. A reminder of this hangs in the Kumbum Monastery, several hundred miles north of Amnemachin, where colorful old murals depict triumphant scenes of hunters displaying dead snow leopards draped over poles.[2]

Overgrazing and hunting pressure, the two factors that account for the decimation of wildlife, are interrelated; the contraction of wildlife habitat by overgrazing means that it is far easier for hunters to find and kill animals. But in a sense, they are both only superficial reasons for the losses. The underlying reasons for the increases in domestic herd size and accelerated hunting are political and economic in nature.

With entrance to a cash economy as a lure, the Ngologs have been actively encouraged by the Chinese government to build up the sizes of their sheep and yak herds. Talking to one Communist party official in Machin,[3] the nearest sizable town to Amnemachin, we learned that the Ngologs' herds have increased roughly tenfold since the Chinese takeover of the region in the late 1950s. Today, a typical nomad will be responsible for about 500 head of sheep and perhaps 20 yaks. More than any other single factor, this expansion of herds has been responsible for the eradication of wildlife and, more generally, for changing drastically the ecological character of the landscape. The soil suffers direct damage from more hoofs than the land can tolerate, as well as an unexpected indirect effect. In this part of the world, where virtually no

2. This monastery is in active use today, with several dozen devotees practicing Buddhism around the clock. Among its other artistic treasures, besides the murals, is a massive Buddha, carved out of butter, that keeps its cool in an inner sanctum of the monastery cellar.

3. Machin is the city's Tibetan name; its Chinese name is Dawu. Generally, I use Tibetan names here, unless otherwise specified.

trees are available for fence materials, the herders make winter enclosures for the sheep out of piled up sod ripped right off the steep slopes. These enclosures are typically four feet high and several hundred feet in diameter, and from the scarred sites where the sod is removed, erosion inevitably starts.

But why have the Chinese encouraged larger herds? One reason is obvious. In western China, agricultural crops are difficult to grow. With the exception of barley, which grows well in the high mountains, few crops are cultivated. Mutton is a main staple of the human diet, and sheepskins are a vital source of clothing material. While the former herd sizes were large enough for the nomads, there now exists a new collection of mouths to feed in the region: tens of thousands of Chinese have settled in Qinghai Province since communization. To feed them, larger herds are needed.

A second reason is more subtle. As mentioned earlier, Ngologs put up fierce resistance to communization in the 1950s. The subsistence of the Ngologs is certainly not dependent on larger herds. But their docility is. The Chinese are, in a sense, herding Ngologs, mollifying them with economic incentives. This is possible, of course, only if Ngologs can be convinced that the things money can buy are worthwhile. Apparently, the Chinese have been successful, for to my surprise, I often observed Ngologs with spectacles (many just empty frames, the glass long since broken) and wristwatches (generally as functional as the spectacles).

These two reasons for burgeoning herds—food for the Chinese and domestication of the Ngologs—are closely linked, for the Chinese did not settle the Tibetan Plateau because of its weather. The Chinese are there to suppress future uprisings.

In an even more perverse turn, the Chinese government is accelerating wildlife decimation by encouraging hunting. A few days out on foot from the village of Qamalung (Snow Mountain Commune), we came on a couple of Ngologs who had recently shot a snow leopard and were preparing the skin for sale to the Chinese government. Desperate for foreign exchange, the Communist regime has recently discovered that oil-rich Middle Easterners are equally desperate for snow leopard pelts. A good pelt can fetch up to $100,000 in Western currency. To encourage the slaughter of the leopards, the Chinese offer Ngologs roughly $10 (in yuan, the Chinese currency) as a bounty on each pelt. The bounty for a wolf skin is roughly $7. Claims by Chinese governmental officials that wolf and leopard hunting was necessary to protect domestic herds were refuted by nomadic herdsmen, who communicated to us that losses of sheep and yaks to predators were insignificant compared with losses to extreme cold. This situation contrasts with that in the United States, where vicious and counterproductive "predator control" policies are largely carried out at the instigation of ranchers; the effect is the same, of course.

There is a bitter political irony in the bounty system of reward in Qinghai. In Communist China, the monetary rewards for the labor of an individual generally go to the individual's commune. The commune then redistributes the income and, in principle, ensures that it provides for the welfare of each member. Even the nomadic herders are communized, and sale of yak or sheep to the government yields profits that are divided collectively. But when a Ngolog sells the government a valuable pelt, he gets to keep the bounty as private profit. Of course, there is increasingly less and less opportunity to make such profit, because the leopards and other wild animals have become so rare.

Before setting out on the nearly 2,000-mile train ride from Beijing to the Tibetan Plateau, we had talked with a variety of Chinese scientists about what to expect in the way of wildlife near Amnemachin and where to find certain species that we were particularly eager to see. One, in particular, was the black-necked crane, a spectacular and endangered bird of which perhaps only a hundred or so remain, all on the Tibetan Plateau. We were assured that we would see one of the few remaining nesting colonies alongside Kora Nor, a lake that lies between Amenmachin to the south and Koko Nor, China's great salt lake, to the north. When we approached the promised area, all we could see, stretching from one horizon to the other, were sheep—vast herds that would have trampled the eggs of any cranes foolish enough to still nest there. The wildlife experts back in Beijing knew far more about political restrictions on our movements than on what wildlife to expect where.

The white-lipped deer is another animal of the Tibetan Plateau whose fate is now in the hands of the Chinese and the Ngologs. A scent gland in the crotch of the deer is believed by the Chinese to confer potency in men, and so, in the apothecaries of Beijing and other major cities, vast amounts of deer extract are sold. The wild population would never be able to sustain such pressure, but, fortunately, the Chinese have begun to raise the deer in large enclosures, thus reducing pressure to hunt the remaining wild deer. Outside the village of Qamalung, we saw one such deer farm; here was a hopeful sign that, with a little ingenuity, at least one animal could be saved.

Although every sight and sound in the plateau is fascinating, I went there with a specific scientific goal. A controversy existed in the late 1970s over just what the acid level of rain would be if there were no pollution. Some spokespersons for polluting industries claimed that even in the absence of pollution, rain would be acidic and acid rain was not really of human origin. Now, in one sense, that is true: rain would be acidic even if there were no pollution because the natural carbon dioxide in the air dissolves in raindrops and makes carbonic acid. But this is a mild acid that could not produce the intensely acid rain found in many parts of the world.

One way to find out if there are other, stronger, natural acids would be to go to very remote regions of the world, far from sources of pollution, and measure the acidity of rain. An obvious place to go to get away from air pollution is the midocean. Unfortunately, however, there are natural oceanic sources of acidity that can render rain acidic over the remote oceans. The source of this natural acidity is sulfur emitted from the sea in sea spray. The sulfuric acid this produces in rain is not of concern, ecologically, because most of it just falls back in the sea and does not affect rain chemistry very much in the acid-sensitive lakes and forests of the world.

Of more interest to me was the quality of the rain in remote *inland* areas, for if rain there were highly acidic, then perhaps the acids falling over North America and Europe could, indeed, be of natural origin as well. Or perhaps acids from the industrialized nations are being carried through the atmosphere all the way to central Asia. In either case, it would be an exciting finding. Where on earth would you go to get as far from pollution as possible, yet still remain inland? A look at a map of the world convinced me that central Asia was the best bet. Amnemachin is thousands of miles from any major upwind industrial area. An expedition led by the mountaineer and photographer, Galen Rowell, afforded me the opportunity to go there; the East-West Center in Honolulu, a research institute dedicated to scientific and cultural studies in the Asia-Pacific region, funded my travel. So off I went.

The first rainstorm that I encountered in the Tibetan Plateau occurred at night in Machin, a town of approximately 30,000 inhabitants, located eighty miles before the road's end at Qamalung where the trail to Amnemachin begins. We were holed up there in an army barracks because an avalanche had blocked the road to Amnemachin, and we had to wait for the Chinese army to clear the way. The rain sample I collected that night had a pH of 2.25 (see chart on page 59), which meant it was the most acidic rainstorm ever recorded in the world—about one hundred times more acidic than the typical rain that falls in the northeastern United States. So much for showing that rain in remote areas is not acidic! The results, however, told me nothing about what I wanted to learn—the acidity of the natural background—because, in fact, the town emitted immense amounts of air pollution.

The source of this rain's intense acidity, in a moderate-sized town far from any industrial center, is local coal burning. At approximately 12,500 feet, temperatures dropped at night to freezing when I sampled the rain, even though it was June. Moreover, the town's sewage polluted its water supply, so all drinking water had to be boiled. Hence, a good deal of coal was continuously burned in the communes not just for warmth but to maintain a vital supply of hot, potable water—a "tea on tap" system.

The type of coal and the way it was burned also contributed to the pollution. The coal was laden with nitrogen and sulfur, both of which end up as acids when the coal is burned. The coal stoves used in Machin, indeed, in most of China, for both heating and cooking are extremely inefficient.

To add to the problem, Machin is afflicted with frequent atmospheric inversions, which means that a stagnant layer of air, in which pollutants concentrate, often hovers above the city. This atmospheric condition, although mainly associated with the sea-level city of Los Angeles, actually plagues many high mountain towns and cities. Finally, the heavy pall of soot produced from the coal burning stimulates the formation of rain because rain droplets tend to form around little soot particles. The town was creating its own private rainstorm, which washed its pollutants back down on itself.

I obtained additional rain samples during a ten-day trek around Amnemachin (following the pilgrimage route), at sites that truly were remote from pollution sources. At those sites, the rain was not acid at all; in fact, it was slightly alkaline. There was not even a trace of the slight level of natural acidity found in most rain in remote areas. Why?

The reason has to do with seashells. Until about fifty million years ago, what is now the Tibetan Plateau was underwater. As the Indian subcontinent drifted northward and collided with central Asia, the crust of the earth under the intervening sea buckled and rose. Thus were the highest mountains in the world today formed, and thus they are still rising. Like almost any present or past coastal seafloor, the newly formed land surface was frosted with a layer of seashell shards many hundreds of feet thick.

Put a drop of battery acid on a pulverized seashell, and you will see it fizz and bubble. The acid is being neutralized by the chalky calcium carbonate that makes up the seashell; the bubbles contain carbon dioxide. Soils containing carbonate-bearing minerals are called alkaline soils. They occur throughout the Great Basin of the western United States and in many other deserts of the world. Nearly every landmass on earth was under the sea at some time in its geologic history, but the places receiving the most rain will have most of their seashell debris eroded away by water. In dry areas, the dust of seashells lingers.

The winds that perpetually roar across the plateau scour the soils, wafting the alkaline dust to the atmosphere. There it dissolves in rain, neutralizing the natural acid and even making it slightly alkaline. Even if the rains were not rendered alkaline by the wind-blown dust, they would have little impact on life in the high plateau. For when the most intensely acid rains, like those at Machin, fall on such highly alkaline soils, they are instantly neutralized and do not harm life in rivers, lakes, or grasslands. In the northeastern United States and the Colorado Rockies, the situation is different. There, in the catchments of some lakes and ponds, the rains fall on acid-sensitive soils, as we saw in chapter 3.

Today's oceans, as well as those of many millions of years ago, affect life in the high Tibetan Plateau. Mountaintop ecosystems would become infertile over time as nutrients wash downhill with the snowmelt unless some source replenishes them. It seems likely that in the high Himalayas, the sparse plant growth is sustained by nutrients from the sea brought in with the monsoonal rain and snow.

The monsoons themselves exist, in part, because of the plateau. At an average elevation of roughly three miles, the vast Tibetan Plateau squats high above the rest of Asia and exerts a major influence on wind patterns. Because land absorbs sunlight more effectively than air, the plateau in spring and summer is warmer than the air would be at that elevation in its absence. Since warm air rises, this results in intense updrafts; to fill the partial vacuum created by the updraft, high altitude, moisture-laden air from the south rushes in toward the plateau, bringing the monsoons to these lands. In addition, the plateau acts like a physical barrier to the prevailing westerly winds at lower elevations, causing them to be diverted to one side. Even far downwind of the plateau, this disturbance causes a persistent effect on air currents that influences weather conditions all around the Northern Hemisphere. A similar but less intense blockage of westerlies occurs in the western United States where the Sierra Nevada of California, the Great Basin, and the southern Rockies form a wind barrier that averages a mile in elevation.

On a longer time scale, the global climatic influence of the Tibetan Plateau may be even more dramatic. The present era of glaciation appears to have begun about the same time as the plateau began its period of most rapid uplift, about twenty million years ago. Throughout the entire period of the plateau's existence, the world has been, on average, cooler than it was during the previous hundreds of millions of years when, to our knowledge, glacial epochs did not exist.

There are a number of proposed explanations for this connection, though none is substantiated. Recall the discussion in our walk up Hidden Creek of how surface ice and snow influence climate by reflecting sunlight and thereby cooling the region (called the ice-albedo effect). As the Tibetan Plateau rose above the relatively sweltering earth of fifty million years ago, it may have become the first major nonpolar region of the planet to sport a snowy surface. If so, it would have decreased the total amount of sunlight absorbed at the earth's surface and thereby exerted a global cooling effect. Eventually, as the plateau rose higher and higher, it perhaps triggered the era of glaciation.

Another argument linking the plateau to the era of glaciation is based on computer simulations of the uplifted landmass's effect on prevailing westerly winds; such simulations, carried out by William Ruddiman of Columbia University and John Kutzbach of the University of Wisconsin, indicate that the winds blow more from the north in much of the Northern Hemisphere when the westerlies are partially blocked by the protruding landmass. Yet another process by which the formation of the plateau could have triggered a cooler climate worldwide has been proposed by Maureen Raymo of the Massachusetts Institute of Technology. She has suggested that as the landmass rose and rain runoff percolated down its slopes, those seashells we discussed earlier began to dissolve in the weak carbonic acid found naturally in the rain. The effect of this is to remove from the atmosphere the carbon dioxide that forms the carbonic acid, sending it down the slopes into the sea dissolved along with calcium from the seashells. With less carbon dioxide, the climate would cool worldwide, an antigreenhouse effect.

Less speculative is the current geographic role of snowfall in the plateau. Amnemachin rises from the eastern side of the plateau's Kunlun mountain range, and the snow falling in these mountains is the source of three of the world's most important rivers—the Mekong, the Yangtze, and the Yellow. Elsewhere on the Tibetan Plateau fall the snows that are the sources of the Indus, the Brahmaputra, the Ganges, the Hong, and the Salween rivers. An astounding 40 percent of the world's population lives in the drainages of the rivers that originate on the plateau, depending on them for irrigation water and fearing their floodwaters.

During the next fifty to one hundred years, if the pace of global warming is not reduced by weaning the world off fossil fuels, the snow and ice on the Tibetan Plateau are likely to exert yet another kind of impact on humanity—one that has the makings of a massive tragedy for these downstream people. Amplified by the ice-albedo effect, global warming will be particularly great in the plateau and will probably cause flooding of the heavily populated downstream valleys as snow and glacial ice melt. With global warming, the snows that now fall on the plateau will be partially replaced with rains. Whether the total volume of precipitation will be more or less than it is today is unknown, but rain on the plateau will be of less use to downstream water users than is today's snow because much of it will evaporate from the plateau before it can enter the river channels. Hence, in the aftermath of flooding may come drought.

But we do not have to wait fifty years to see the human consequences of tampering with the ecological life support system. Let us follow one of the rivers originating on the plateau, the Yellow, as it flows through north central China to the ocean just east of Beijing. Returning from the Amnemachin expedition to Beijing, we did just that on a nearly 2,000-mile train ride. As the river starts to level out at the edge of the plateau, its waters make the transition from the chalky gray of glacial melt to a smoggy-colored brownish yellow that gives it its name. The color is derived from the eroding soils of the region. Here, the forests, whose foliage once broke the force of the rain and whose roots held the soil in place, are gone. Instead, fields of wheat, corn, and other staple crops of north central China stretch from the riverbanks to the terraced tops of the foothills. Here, also, flooding of the Yellow River occurs regularly, with flood intensity exacerbated in part by deforestation and in part by loss of stream channel as increasing amounts of eroded material silt up the riverbed. The toll on human life wrought by flooding of the Yellow and similar rivers in China is severe, with hundreds of thousands of people killed just in the past several decades.

Erosion is increasing in China. While intense deforestation and tillage have undoubtedly contributed to this, just how large a role they play is uncertain. One estimate is that, throughout China, agricultural practices coupled with deforestation have resulted in five billion tons of soil washing to the sea each year, or blowing away in the wind.[4] If so, this means that China, occupying 7 percent of the world's land area, is responsible for about 25 percent of all human-caused erosion. More important for its people, it means that China is losing its topsoil so fast that if this trend continues, then in a few more decades this vital resource will be seriously depleted and agricultural productivity will plummet.

The magnitude of the problem is hard to estimate. The Yellow River was named thousands of years ago, and so, clearly, erosion is not new to north central China. In fact, the yellowish soils of the region, called loess, are blown in from the Mongolian steppes to the north. We do not really know to what extent soil loss to the Yellow River is replaced by soil "import" from Mongolia. And we also do not know to what extent wind erosion from Mongolia may be increasing because of land use practices there.

Similar confusion surrounds the status of soil erosion in the Nepalese Himalayan foothills. A widely held view is that deforestation and overly intense cultivation of the Himalayan slopes have been responsible for massive erosion and flooding, leading even to the occasional inundation of the northern plains of India by the floodwaters of the Ganges and other rivers that originate on the south slopes of the Himalaya. More recently, Jack Ives of the University of California, Davis, and other scientists have questioned this prevailing view, arguing that there are not enough data to support it and that the land use practices of the Sherpas are ecologically better than Western scientists generally believe.[5]

4. The source of this estimate is *The Bad Earth,* by Vaclav Smil (London: Zed Press, 1984). This book, which discusses air and water pollution as well as loss of forests and soil erosion, paints an exceedingly bleak picture of the state of the Chinese environment.

5. See, for example, J. Ives and B. Messerri, *The Himalayan Dilemma: Reconciling Development and Conservation* (London: Routledge, 1989).

Water in China carries more than topsoil, unfortunately. As in Machin, water is unfit to drink throughout most of China. This is not simply the experience of squeamish Western visitors with sensitive stomachs, for even the Chinese boil their water before drinking it, whether it is used for tea or not. The reason is that raw sewage is often dumped untreated on the land, from whence it enters the groundwater that feeds the wells, or it goes straight into rivers, a major source of domestic water in China.

Many forms of pollution are not eliminated by boiling, of course, and these, too, pose a serious health threat. They include nitrates from agricultural runoff, which, once ingested, can turn into cancer-causing nitrosamines,[6] and numerous organic chemicals and heavy metals, like mercury and iron, from industry.

The problem of nitrate poisoning is exacerbated by erosion. Each year, thirty million tons of nitrogen, much of it in organic form and therefore not toxic to humans, washes out of the hills above the Yellow River and flows downstream. To replace this loss, the Chinese have turned to industrial fertilizers and thereby have increased the nitrate levels in well water.

Another ripple effect of erosion is that energy from coal is expended to make these fertilizers. The topic of energy is increasingly in the forefront of public policy in China today, just as it became so in the United States in the mid-1970s. Even high on the plateau, we could not escape witnessing how energy is linked to political and social issues. On the 500-mile drive south from Xining to Snow Mountain Commune, on a seemingly deserted muddy mountain road, we found ourselves at one point in a miasma of truck fumes with no source in sight. Soon, however, we passed a convoy of about fifty trucks creeping south to Lhasa, the capital of Tibet. They were carrying petroleum to supply the Chinese soldiers, party functionaries, and others emplaced there to solidify Chinese hegemony in this isolated land. Driving steadily for eight days over tortuous roads to deliver the oil to Lhasa, and then back again to Xining, they burn nearly half of the fuel they start out with. This is

6. The connection between nitrates and esophageal cancer was discovered in China, as have many other dietary causes of diseases. China has been able to pioneer this type of study for several reasons. First, the Chinese are, relatively speaking, a genetically homogeneous people with diverse regional food customs. Second, the people do not generally move from one region to another, and thus their exposures to regional carcinogens remain fairly constant over time. Third, the government collects very comprehensive data on the incidence of diseases.

only one small example of the many prices the Chinese pay for the privilege of subjugating a nation.

Using the issue of energy scarcity as a bugaboo, Communist party officials in Qinghai, who resent the survival of Buddhism, have claimed the monasteries are using too much energy and should be shut down. Turning from the ridiculous to the consequential, however, the Chinese government has concluded that its ambitious economic development plans will only be possible with a vast expansion of coal consumption. China does possess considerable petroleum resources, located offshore, and in principle could harvest this cleaner fuel for domestic use. But the government has chosen coal to fuel its planned economic expansion, setting aside the petroleum for sale overseas to thus bring in much-needed hard currency from the West.

Plans are now under way for a doubling of Chinese coal consumption by the year 2000 and for far greater increases during the early years of the next millennium. If these ambitious plans are achieved, China will probably become the world's largest coal consumer and its largest producer of climate-altering carbon dioxide.[7] On a per capita basis, however, China will still be using less energy and producing less carbon dioxide than does the United States or Europe. How are we in the West to tell China that it does not have the right to develop economically, using the same cheap and dirty fuels that got us to the lofty economic perch where we now selfishly sit?

With about one-third of the world's coal lying in its lands, China certainly has the geologic resources to achieve her goal. Less clear is whether China possesses big enough "sinks" for all its "dirt," that is, the air and water within which to dilute the pollution produced from burning such a vast amount of coal, or the technical and economic resources needed to burn the coal cleanly. On a main thoroughfare in Beijing, lined gracefully with poplars and plane trees, a huge truck cruises daily, pumping water on the trees to wash off the pollutants. This Chinese-style "scrubber" is, of course, no substitute for scrubbers

7. Currently, China is the world's third-largest CO_2 producer. In 1990, China consumed roughly the same amount of coal as the United States but only about one-third as much total energy. This simply reflects the major role of petroleum and natural gas in the United States. Chinese development plans do include an increase in noncoal energy sources as well. In 1990, there were about 3 million cars and trucks in China, but the government plans to increase that to 13 million by the year 2000. On a per-person basis, the Chinese currently consume only about one-tenth as much energy as do people in Western Europe, Japan, and the United States.

installed in factories or for more efficient stoves and furnaces. Water can be used for cosmetic purposes along a showpiece street, but the water does not exist in China to clean all the trees and crops at risk from air pollution. And the human respiratory tract cannnot be washed clean of the air pollutants that assault it daily, whether in the major Chinese cities or the outlying towns like Machin.

At a scientific meeting in Beijing in 1983, I was pleased to learn that the Chinese were beginning to study acid rain, that my work in the Tibetan Plateau was well known to them, and that insights from Western acid rain research were being discussed. I was less pleased to recognize the tremendous gulf between what they mean by pollution standards and what we in the West mean. In China, the term "pollution standard" means a prediction, not an enforceable limit. They calculate what pollution levels are likely to be under plausible assumptions about fuel consumption and meager government spending on pollution control. They call the result of the calculation a "standard." If it is exceeded, it is not the factories that get the blame; it is the person who worked out the estimate. It took the better part of a morning-long and confusing scientific session at the meeting before this cultural difference became apparent and productive conversation could ensue.

A presentation by my Berkeley colleague Arthur Rosenfeld on the enormous potential for energy conservation appeared to win over some Chinese converts later that day. China, like other developing nations, has tended to view economic development as being synonymous with increased energy consumption. In the industrialized nations, the evidence has become overwhelming that improvements in energy efficiency can fuel economic growth just as effectively as can new energy sources. Indeed, many scientists who study this issue believe that the only way developing nations can significantly improve their standard of living and their "gross national product" is to do so by avoiding the energy- and money-wasteful mistakes made in countries like the United States.

Prior to 1973, energy use in the United States grew roughly in step with economic growth, as measured by gross national product (GNP). Many people thought that this relation between energy and GNP was an inevitable one. But, from 1973 to 1981, the United States' GNP rose 30 percent while energy consumption remained virtually constant. Why? Because tighter fuel efficiency standards for cars and numerous other energy conservation measures led to a more efficient economy.

Even though energy prices rose in the United States, the people saved several hundred billion dollars during that period by not wasting money on wasted energy.

Ironically and sadly, during the Reagan and Bush administrations, energy efficiency was virtually abandoned as a domestic goal, and we no longer set the good example of a decade earlier. It is not at all clear if the developing nations will do as we do or as our more enlightened scientists, engineers, and economists say we should do.

The conference marked the first serious dialogue between China and the West on the issue of energy conservation. With any luck, it will lead to a change in the direction of China's energy policy, emphasizing the value of increasing the energy efficiency of the society and not just its energy consumption.

While the conference focused primarily on industrial uses of energy, where the Chinese feel government action can have the biggest impact, the opportunities for improved energy efficiency may actually be greatest in the home. In China, as in much of the world, significant reductions in fuel use could be achieved with improved stove design. As if that were not reason enough, an added incentive is that levels of indoor air pollution could be greatly reduced with stove design improvements.

Two incidents in Qinghai province brought home to me the seriousness of the problem and the possibility of solutions in unexpected quarters. In Machin, we were put up for the night in an empty army commune; each room had a glowing coal fire in a little metal stove used for warmth and for tea preparation. At night, the fumes from the stove in my room were suffocating, but attempts to alleviate the problem by opening the window simply caused the even more polluted (and frigid) air in the commune courtyard, where the stovepipes vented, to get sucked into the sleeping quarters.

A week later, on foot around Amnemachin, I noticed a peculiar object on the ground. Clearly made by hand from baked earth, it was a sloping trough with a raised, open-top chamber at the lower end. A few miles later, we came on another and soon noticed that they were scattered around the landscape, despite the absence of any other signs of human life. A few days later, when we stumbled on a nomadic Ngolog family living in a yurt, we learned just how cleverly designed these homemade stoves were. The stoves are located where the nomads can hope to find adequate grass for their sheep and yak herds. When a nomadic family wants to settle down for a few months, they simply place their yurt, with a hole in the top to vent fumes, on top of one of these stoves. To burn animal dung (the only fuel available), the Ngologs load the dung at the top of the trough and let the heat of the fire dry it out. As the dung dries, it is easy to roll or push it down the trough to the fire at the lower end. The smoke is drawn up the chamber, and, miraculously, it heads straight for the opening in the yak skin eight feet above.

At the kind invitation of the family, we spent a delightful three hours sitting with them around the stove in the yurt, with the door flap closed for warmth, sharing barley and yak butter soup and attempting conversation. The air was fine in the yurt, although the soup took a little getting used to. The stove would undoubtedly work terribly in a commune in Machin or an apartment in Beijing. But it was beautifully designed for the type of fuel it used and for the dwelling in which it was located.

"Synergy" is a term much in vogue today with earth's friends. It is one of those words, like "organic," that bulldozes away all caveats in its path. Synergism is ecologically beneficial and healthful to society. It is on the side of Buckminster Fuller and his angels. With it, we are in good hands. It means, literally, a uniting of energies, a teaming up. Synergy can, indeed, lead to a whole that is better than the sum of its parts, to an entity that is better able to withstand stress than could the individual components. The human body is a perfect example: what good is the kidney without the lungs, the brain without the liver?

Ecosystems offer slightly less obvious examples: the wood storks and alligators of the Everglades, the salmon and the lichen in Alaska, the denizens of coral reefs. In a healthy ecosystem, these synergies are the guts of what we mean by the hackneyed phrase, "the balance of nature." On a continental or global scale, the synergies are quite hidden from casual view but no less important. Microorganisms that produce gases that, in turn, regulate the stratospheric ozone layer depend on habitats maintained by plants; those plants would be injured if a greatly increased amount of ultraviolet radiation peppered the earth as a result of the thinning of the stratospheric ozone layer. Climate on a vast regional scale is influenced by tropical forests whose growth is conditioned by that climate.

Some people have taken the superficial resemblance between global interactions and the linkages among the organs of the body as evidence that the entire planetary biosphere is protected against stress the way an individual organism is. Called the Gaia hypothesis by James Lovelock, a leading advocate of the idea, this picture of an alive planet makes for lovely imagery. Unfortunately, it is not a hypothesis that can be tested within the framework of science because it is impossible to disprove it; it can happily digest all facts and adapt itself to them. By "explaining" everything, it provides no useful explanation of anything.[8]

The rosy picture painted by Gaia enthusiasts ignores the sinister side of synergy. When a body is in good health, the links among its components often work well together. What else would you expect from a system that evolved to its present form through trial and error? But consider the situation that a hospitalized patient having major surgery faces. There is risk of infection from a blood transfusion or from other hospital patients. There is the hazard to the heart and the nuisance of bedsores from remaining bedridden for weeks, the stress on the entire system from the anesthesia. Administered painkillers may cause allergic reactions or elevate blood pressure and thereby cause internal bleeding. In other words, under stresses that differ dramatically from those that shaped the evolution of the organism, the once beneficially synergistic links can magnify rather than mute the damage.

At a global level, an analogous phenomenon occurs. Humanity is now stressing the entire planetary life support system by cutting down vast areas of forest, draining wetlands, and placing chlorofluorocarbons in the stratosphere, acids in lakes and soils, carbon dioxide in the atmosphere, and toxic metals in the waterways. These are not exactly the sorts of stresses to which ecosystems were subjected when the links within and between these systems were forged over evolutionary and geologic time scales. In the case of the chlorofluorocarbons, the stress is unprecedented because these ozone-destroying chemicals are synthetic. In the case of the buildup of climate-altering carbon dioxide in the atmosphere, the uniqueness of the stress comes from the intensity or rapidity of the anticipated impacts. While temperature changes of 4 to 9 degrees Fahrenheit are not unprecedented in the record of geologic climate history, rarely did such warming occur over a period of a mere fifty years. And the species extinction rate that tropical deforestation is triggering, estimated to be in the range of thousands or perhaps tens

8. For a description of Gaia by its chief proponents and a critique of the notion that the Gaia hypothesis is a scientific hypothesis, see the collection of essays in *Scientists on Gaia,* edited by S. Schneider and P. Boston (Cambridge: MIT Press, 1991).

of thousands of species per year, far exceeds the natural extinction rate, which is probably closer to about one species per year except in the unusual event of asteroid impacts.

Under these extraordinary stresses, the links that form life-sustaining synergies under natural conditions turn against the health of the system as they amplify, rather than dampen, stress. Consider the following examples. While global warming will warm earth's surface, it will actually cool the stratosphere, increasing ice-cloud formation there. These ice clouds speed up stratospheric ozone depletion by providing solid surfaces that strongly promote the major ozone-depleting reactions. Thus, the greenhouse effect will worsen the problem of stratospheric ozone depletion. At the same time, greenhouse warming at the earth's surface will make the urban ozone pollution problem worse by speeding up the chemical reactions that lead to smog formation.

Global climate warming will also increase the threat of insect pests and disease vectors. To see why, recall that a number of insect pests that destroy crops in temperate latitudes are held in check by wintertime cold snaps. Reduce the frequency or severity of cold snaps, and you will likely see population explosions of such pests. The tropics and subtropics are home to a far greater variety of diseases than the colder regions of the globe. Numerous disease vectors, like the *Anopheles* mosquito that carries malaria or the tsetse fly that carries sleeping sickness, are confined to the tropics and subtropics because of their intolerance to cold. As the planet warms, it is quite likely that the ranges of many tropical disease carriers will spread poleward. And in the tropics, climate warming will act in concert with deforestation to accelerate loss of forest, as we saw from the discussion of mahogany trees in chapter 5.

Consider, next, the stress of deforestation. It will add to the threat of greenhouse warming, by releasing carbon dioxide to the atmosphere as felled trees rot or are burned. It also generates acid rain, as has been observed in Africa where nitric acid is formed from burning vegetation. Stratospheric ozone depletion will probably lead to more intense smog because the additional ultraviolet radiation penetrating a thinned stratospheric ozone layer will speed up the chemical reactions that produce smog.

And to top it off, plants and animals weakened by any one of these threats will generally be more vulnerable to the others. There are numerous examples of this. Fish weakened by radiation have been shown to be more easily damaged by thermal pollution than are healthy fish, and trees subjected to some air pollutants become more susceptible to insect damage.

Just as these destructive synergies offer little hope for Gaia-like robustness on the global scale, the case of China illustrates well how synergies can inexorably undermine health on a more local scale, for China is plagued with an ecosystem of predicaments. Drinking water contaminated with pathogens must be boiled, thus requiring the use of more energy. This energy is produced with dirty fuels burned with inadequate pollution control because of a dismal balance of payments situation and an economy that cannot provide surplus for environmental "luxuries," such as petroleum rather than coal, because it can barely keep up with population growth. The resulting air pollutants lead to health problems and loss of economic productivity as well as great expectorations in crowded city streets, thereby spreading disease. Inadequate sewage facilities further contaminate the water. Destruction of forests for more cropland, fuel wood, and construction material, all for a growing population, leads to more erosion, loss of agricultural productivity, and increased demand for fertilizers. More fertilizer use further pollutes water and requires more fossil fuel and further drains the economy.[9] In this tapestry, each frayed thread chafes against and wears its neighbors.

Despite the bleak picture of China's environmental health painted here, there are reasons for hope. China has solved many social problems with an effectiveness that seems almost incomprehensible to foreigners. While it has come at terrible cost to the land, China is able to feed a billion people with a diet that is adequate and perhaps even healthier than that of the developed (more accurately, the overdeveloped) nations. While it has come at a terrible cost to individual freedoms, crime and lesser public nuisances that plague the West have been reduced to a relatively low level.

And, ultimately most encouraging of all, China is starting to come to grips with the problem of population growth. Using intense educa-

9. Two and a half thousand years ago, Confucius exhorted the peasantry and particularly the rural bureaucracy to pay attention to synergies—both the good kind and the bad kind. He knew that water, soil, plant cover, and climate were linked to each other and could promote productivity and health; he also described how, if they were maltreated, deterioration would set in rapidly and inexorably. In short, he understood the concept of "nature's services." His message, it appears, is not outdated.

tional campaigns, social peer pressure, and undoubtedly some physical constraints, China's one-child-family campaign is lowering the population growth rate, even though exceptions to the policy are numerous. This, not the Communist Revolution of the 1940s, is the true Chinese revolution—a revolution in thinking that will eventually have more beneficial impact on the quality of life for more people around the world than any conventional revolution.[10]

The temptation exists to conclude that these partial successes in China are simply due to thought control and dictatorial exercise of army-backed governmental authority, yet it would be a mistake to ignore the role of history and cultural tradition. On the long train ride from Xining back to Beijing along the Yellow River, I saw endless networks of irrigation ditches leading from the river to the wheat fields and other croplands of north central China. At various places along this network, where a main branch forked or even where a minor split occurred far removed from a main branch, I saw a Chinese peasant wearing a straw hat, sitting, ready to turn a wheel that slowed or sped the flow of water, or to divert it to the right or left. I later learned that the system works splendidly, and over an area of thousands of square miles, thousands of peasants maintain flows where needed, and avoid floods when possible, throughout the whole complex network. I did not learn how information was transmitted and processed there. Do the gate operators get their signals from the magnitude of the flows? Surely they were not following some rigid formula. In the West, we would communicate electronically with each operator in the network, probably from a centralized computer facility.

It is a cliché that in China, more than in the West, the individual perceives his or her relation to the larger community as one of compo-

10. Party Chairman Mao actually opposed birth control, labeling it "bourgeois Malthusian doctrine" during the 1950s and 1960s; current population policies in China were formulated after his death. To reduce the rate of population growth, other nations have set, or will set, different goals and use different incentives, but the dramatic shift in thinking that has taken place in China will inevitably take hold elsewhere. As the opportunities for education increase and the status of women improves in poor countries, desire for smaller families will increase. Then, if governments encourage small families and the use of birth control, the more coercive policies adopted by China will not be necessary. I am as distressed as anyone by reports of forced abortions in China and hope that the reports are false. But I cannot help but wonder whether, with respect to this issue, a government that denies women the right to reproductive freedom and the medical opportunities to exercise that right is acting any less dictatorially than is one that approaches population growth as China does, with its own style of abridgment of reproductive freedom.

nent rather than opponent. For thousands of years, this relationship has been embodied in China's literature and custom.[11] Taking advantage of the social cohesiveness of the people and of strong traditions of thrift and husbandry, the Communists have been able to harness and magnify the individual's effort in ways that seem antlike to Westerners.

The operation of the Yellow River irrigation network illustrates the effectiveness of culture and technology working together. But progress in China has come about under a totalitarian regime that, on the one hand, exploited and, on the other hand, strove to eliminate much of the socially responsible traditions in China. By undermining the very foundation of its success, the Communists are probably ensuring tough times ahead for the Chinese people. The backlash of greed and crime that accompanied the brief loosening up of the economy in the mid-1980s indicates that the short-term successes of the Communist regime may be paving the way for long-term troubles. The savage events in Tian'anmen Square in June 1989 provide only the most dramatic example of how the public trust can be easily betrayed. A cynical and uncooperative Chinese people may be the long-term legacy of communism.

We journeyed a long way from the Ngologs and the snow leopards of Qinghai Province, for only downstream could we discern the synergistic forces acting to disintegrate their land and society. And by looking farther beyond China to the world's oceans, atmosphere, forests, and climate, where similarly destructive synergies operate, we saw how the seemingly remote Tibetan Plateau is truly next door.

Back on the plateau, it strains the imagination at first to connect that peaceable Ngolog family embarking on their 100-mile pilgrimage around sacred Amnemachin with the nomadic "people with their heads on backward" who fought the Chinese army to a near standstill in the 1950s. But there probably is a common wellspring to both Ngolog dedication to religious rites and the Ngolog propensity to slaughter in-

11. There are, as of course there must be, delightful exceptions. The Thoreau-like twelfth-century curmudgeon, Tao Chien, is my favorite. In middle age, he thumbed his nose at society and went off to the woods to drink rice wine, delight in the flight of birds, and write splendid poetry.

truders; it is the toughness and resolve needed to live under the harsh conditions of nomadic life in the Tibetan Plateau.

Although the Chinese were never able to forcibly eliminate the Ngologs' religious practices, they probably will achieve that goal by other means. Wandering peoples like the nomads of the Sahel, the Gypsies of southern Europe, the Aboriginals of Australia, and the Ngologs are often the first victims of the environmental and social disintegration wrought by the sedentary. Like the salamander eggs at the Mexican Cut, the nomadic livelihood is permeable to foreign stresses.

The Chinese have used cash incentives to encourage Ngologs to slaughter wildlife and the lure of downstream market produce to encourage expansion of sheep and yak herds beyond the carrying capacity of the land. As the Ngologs are pushed from their traditional nomadic life by the degradation of the land and pulled by the seduction of a cash economy, the odds are that Ngolog culture will disintegrate and Chinese subjugation will be complete. Downstream, vestiges of Confucian wisdom may still nourish human existence in the rice fields, but the only traditions China has introduced into the Tibetan Plateau are those of its imperial past—autocracy and hegemony backed by muscle.

The Ngologs have been captivated, in both senses of the word, by the Chinese. But the empty spectacle frames and the wristwatches frozen in time, for which the Ngologs can thank the Chinese, are no substitute for a lost vision of a snow leopard and a lost opportunity for a sustainable future.

EPILOGUE

Our story began with a migration of salmon from Bristol Bay to their spawning grounds at the headwaters of Hidden Creek and concluded with another migration, that of nomads on a mountain in China where the Yellow River begins. Hidden Creek and the Yellow River seem a world apart, yet their commonality is deep, for they are linked by one atmosphere and one ocean. Although each stream's trajectory yields the illusion that humanity's influences only flow downstream, the engines of the human economy can be heard at both headwaters.

The most important migration of humanity may be just beginning, as we attempt to leave the dried and worn pastures of domination over nature and chart a new path that will take us to a sustainable and healthy future. It is a journey no less bold and challenging than those of the great explorers centuries ago.

Those early explorations would not have been taken by people hanging onto the old notion of a flat earth over whose edge ships would fall; it took a new geography to give birth to a new, edgeless vision of the human potential. Similarly, our forthcoming journey is stalled by another outmoded myth, one that concerns temporal rather than spatial bounds. Let us see how the science we have explored provides some hints of the next "new geography," a geography that might be parent to a timeless, abiding vision of humanity.

Like many scientists, I feel awkward talking about myths and values because they cannot be analyzed with the tools in our kit bag. Nevertheless, science is chock-full of value-laden implications; the often heard statement that science is value-free, that it stands outside of culture, ethics, or morals, is arrant nonsense. For one thing, the prevailing values of a culture influence what scientists choose to study. Second, scientific results feed back into and shape culture, whether scientists like it or not. The myths that provide societies with a conception of themselves are shaped in part by science. Thus, the scientific insights associated with Copernicus, Darwin, and Einstein all influenced the degree of divinity people attach to their planet, their lineage, and their role in the universe, respectively.

In such varied ways, scientific findings fertilize the soil of reason and experience. Here grow our ideas about right and wrong. Consider the golden rule, "Do unto others as you would have others do unto you" (or the earlier Hebraic version, "Do not do to others what you do not want others to do to you"). The rational basis of this rule is a relentless kind of self-consistency. Suppose you are contemplating an action: to test its moral consistency, simply assume others will act the same way. If that leads to a world in which you are content to live, then the action is "right."[1] This rule provides a test of the goodness of any contemplated action, not a list of things you should or should not do. The wisdom that led to its formulation is akin to that of Confucius when he offered the hungry a fishing rod, not a fish.

Experience is also part of the story, for experience leads to knowledge of the kinds of reciprocated actions that will make the world more or less livable; it allows a person to apply the consistency test to any contemplated behavior, and thus it puts flesh on the golden rule's logical skeleton. And at that step, science has something to say about what is right or wrong.

The everyday experiences of the Hebraic and Christian philosophers molded their conception of the types of actions to which the rule could be applied and specified who, for all practical purposes, the term "others" in the golden rule referred to. Murder and theft—evils as old

1. Immanuel Kant whose philosophical journeys often explored the concept of morality, probed deeply into the foundations of this rule. His writings point to the following conclusion. If we include in the actions that we project onto others, the very act of adopting a rule for testing the goodness of our actions, then the golden rule itself has a logical basis (Kant calls such a basis a categorical imperative): "Adopt a rule governing how you deal with others as you would have them adopt a rule for dealing with you." Golden, indeed.

as humanity—were the actions of concern; "others" referred literally to one's neighbors. Since the beginnings of the Industrial Revolution, however, people have increasingly had the technical capability to degrade the lives of their neighbors through actions that the biblical philosophers could not even have imagined. Moreover, they have been able to extend the range of that damage to people worldwide.

The preceding chapters portrayed some of the ways in which we are using that capability to foul the seas and the atmosphere, acidify lakes, alter the climate, dry the wetlands, clear-cut the forests, destroy the ozone shield, erode soils, and extinguish the existence of numerous plant and animal species. Experience clearly dictates that the term "others" in the golden rule encompasses people all over the planet, including those that may never see or know us, if the rational basis of the rule—its self-consistency—is to be retained.[2]

In this age of rapid, worldwide communication, it does not drastically stretch the imagination to extend the golden rule in this way. But we cannot stop here, for the real lesson of our journey from Hidden Creek to Amnemachin is that "others" must include future generations that may be affected by our actions. Nobody would doubt that our actions are affecting the lives of future generations. Every barrel of oil we pump from underground and burn is one less barrel for our descendants to use. Every species and every acre of wilderness that we destroy is one less from which they can benefit. Every ton of topsoil washed to the sea by careless land practices is one less ton in which they can grow food. Every child born today is a potential great-great-grandparent of a legacy of people who will, a century later, occupy space, consume resources, and also will want to create a legacy of great-great-grandchildren.

But how does the golden rule's logic of self-consistency fit in here? While *our* actions will affect future generations, self-consistency seems difficult to apply because *their* actions surely cannot affect us. How can we argue that future generations belong among the "others"? What, in short, can future generations do for, or to, us?

2. I am indebted to the writings of Kenneth Boulding, Christopher Stone, Charles Hartshorne, and especially Robert Heilbroner and Hans Jonas for inspiring the lines of thought above, although my conclusions below differ from theirs. An excellent book on these themes, which contains some of their writings, is *Responsibilities to Future Generations,* edited by E. Partridge (Buffalo: Prometheus Books, 1981). See also *Earth and Other Ethics: The Case for Moral Pluralism,* by C. D. Stone (New York: Harper and Row, 1987).

To continue down this path requires abandoning a cherished myth that underlies the concept of existence in the West and, to some extent, throughout all cultures. This is the myth of individuation—of the separate reality of the pieces of the whole. But I do not mean that one must abandon the notion that individual people have separate existences. While that particular myth of individuation can be questioned—and, in fact, is questioned in some Eastern philosophies—that is not what I have in mind. Rather, we must ponder the question of whether individual segments on the time line of humanity have any useful meaning.

I believe that life on earth, including humanity, can only be consistently and usefully thought of as existing over all of biologic time. The notion of "life at 11:22 A.M. (GMT), November 7, 1990," has no more useful meaning than "life at a point in space." Only a few paltry statistics can describe humanity at a particular moment in time—the size of the human population, the monetary wealth of nations, for example. But such static descriptors cannot capture what we really *are*. We are a process, not a snapshot; a collection of memories and hopes, not a configuration of faces. Where is our humanity if we are not aware of, and wiser because of, our history? And more to the point, where is our humanity if we are not aware of, and caring for, our future? In the absence of such care, we can sustain no hope, and without hope, there is no human existence. The process is over.

If "others" means all of humanity—past, present, and future—then the reinterpreted golden rule regains its elegant self-consistent character. Had our forebears left for us the ecological devastation we are leaving for our descendants, we would not have the options currently available to us for our enjoyment or even long-term survival. Today, we can live wisely on earth and inspire, by example, our descendants to do the same. Or we can continue to destroy the life-supporting fabric of the planet, forcing our descendants to live in a far more desperate fashion because they will not have the luxury of the bountiful resources that we inherited.

The answer to the question, what can future generations do *for* us? is simple. They give us a reason for treating our ecological home respectfully, so that our lives as well as theirs will be enriched. What can they do *to* us? They can project back to us a vision of desperation, futility, the end of hope and life, a vision that will plague our remaining days if we act so as to fulfill that vision by continuing to degrade our planet.

Reverence for the future is a notion that is foreign to virtually all religious beliefs.[3] Ancestor worship, creation tales, how the "this" got its "that" stories, lives of the dead saints—those are the stuff of most religions. Sure, the fate of each of our souls is the subject of much religious dogma. But it is ***our*** souls that are the concern of priests and parishioners alike, not those of our great-great-grandchildren. The conventional eternity is a wishful prolongation of our sentient selves, of us alive now, not a continuing wellspring of life. A religion based on an ecologically defensible vision of our home would not be so shortsighted; it would take all of humanity, past and future, under its wing. What better creation story is there than a reminiscent tale by a frugal grandmother which will be remembered and retold two generations later by a grandmother-to-be. What finer eternity could there be than one in which children always have the opportunity to roam the slopes of Sage Hill?

To think about all of yet unborn humanity, to consider their interests as we contemplate daily actions, is a tall order. Taken too literally, such notions could confound all decision making. But these abstractions actually do translate into razor-sharp arguments that can cut through a good deal of muddled thinking on practical and pressing issues. Here are a few examples:

- When confronted with the frequently made argument that people are a good thing, so let us have more of them (and therefore ban contraception and scuttle family planning programs), we can reply: Yes, let us have as many people on this planet as possible—*but not all at the same time*. Let us populate the world with people for as long into the future as possible, by taking care that we limit population growth now.[4]
- To the argument that the banning of timber cutting in old-growth forests, oil drilling near marine sanctuaries, or strip mining in the wilderness will eliminate existing jobs, we can reply that if those nat-

3. Among the belief systems that express this vision are those attributed to some Native Americans. Consider, for example, the Navajo saying, We do not own land, we borrow it from our children.

4. I am indebted to Herman Daly, the economist famous for developing the notion of a steady state economy, for this rebuttal.

ural resources are left intact, their inherent recreational and ecological value will create and sustain a far greater number of jobs for numerous future generations of workers. However, if these finite resources are mined greedily today, the ephemeral jobs will soon disappear along with the resources, permanently destroying future opportunities for a much greater number of jobs.

- To the argument that we need to extract more rapidly our oil, gas, and coal resources to fuel growth of our industrial society, we can reply that the society that knows only how to burn fuel profligately will soon have none, whereas the society that knows how to use it efficiently can save barrel after barrel, generation after generation. Frugality and efficiency are the gifts that keep on giving.
- To the argument that society faces a choice between the welfare of people and the survival of some obscure fish, flower, fungus, or frog species, we can reply: The well-being of people and the survival of species are synonymous. Sure, in the short run, exterminating a wild species may confer on some people some advantage. But like a quick pickup from a narcotic, this advantage comes at the cost of placing the long-term health of humanity in jeopardy. The loss of every wild species is a loss of opportunity, both economic and aesthetic, for all the generations of our descendants. And the deliberate destruction of a species leaves a scar on the conscience of humanity that will never heal.

It is sometimes said that a major shift of perception occurred when people began to view themselves as the stewards rather than the rulers of nature. This shift, symbolized by the transition from hunter to herder, is sometimes viewed as the beginnings of environmentalism. Maybe. But the metaphor of people as nature's steward leaves me just as dissatisfied as does a temporally bounded vision of humanity. Nature needs no steward. If there is stewardship, nature holds it over us, for the goods and services humanity derives from natural processes truly sustain our existence and are the basis of all civilizations. Without them, we live in economic and spiritual poverty.

But as with those endless philosophical arguments centering on ill-conceived distinctions between mind and body, reason and emotion, so attempts to split apart humanity and nature are ultimately only an invitation to confusion. The economic and spiritual health of humanity is utterly dependent on the health of nature. At the same time, because of our vast numbers and our misdirected technological arsenal, because of our reach into every reef and tropical forest, alpine pond and patch of arctic tundra, wetland and desert, nature is only as enduring as the health of human society. Only when the seeming opposites of chaos and continuity, wilderness and sustainability, are fused within our moral vision and our myths, just as they are fused on the slopes of Sage Hill, will humanity have hope of abiding.

We return, then, as any ecological odyssey must, to where we began, to Dylan Thomas's vision of the unity of life and the commonality of the forces that create and destroy it, for there is no better summary of the journey we have undertaken:

> The force that through the green fuse drives the flower
> Drives my green age; that blasts the roots of trees
> Is my destroyer.

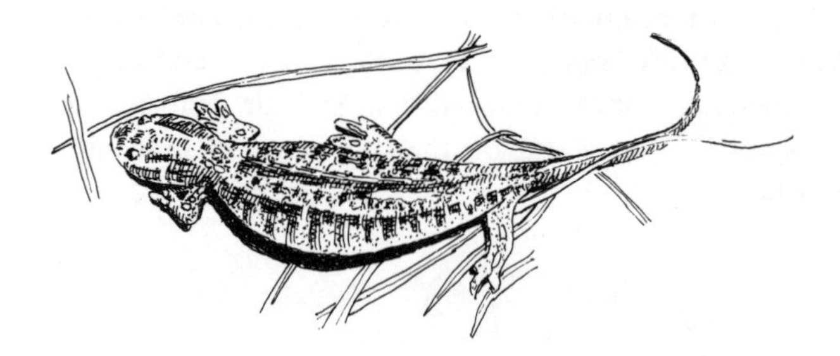

INDEX